Peter Foreman

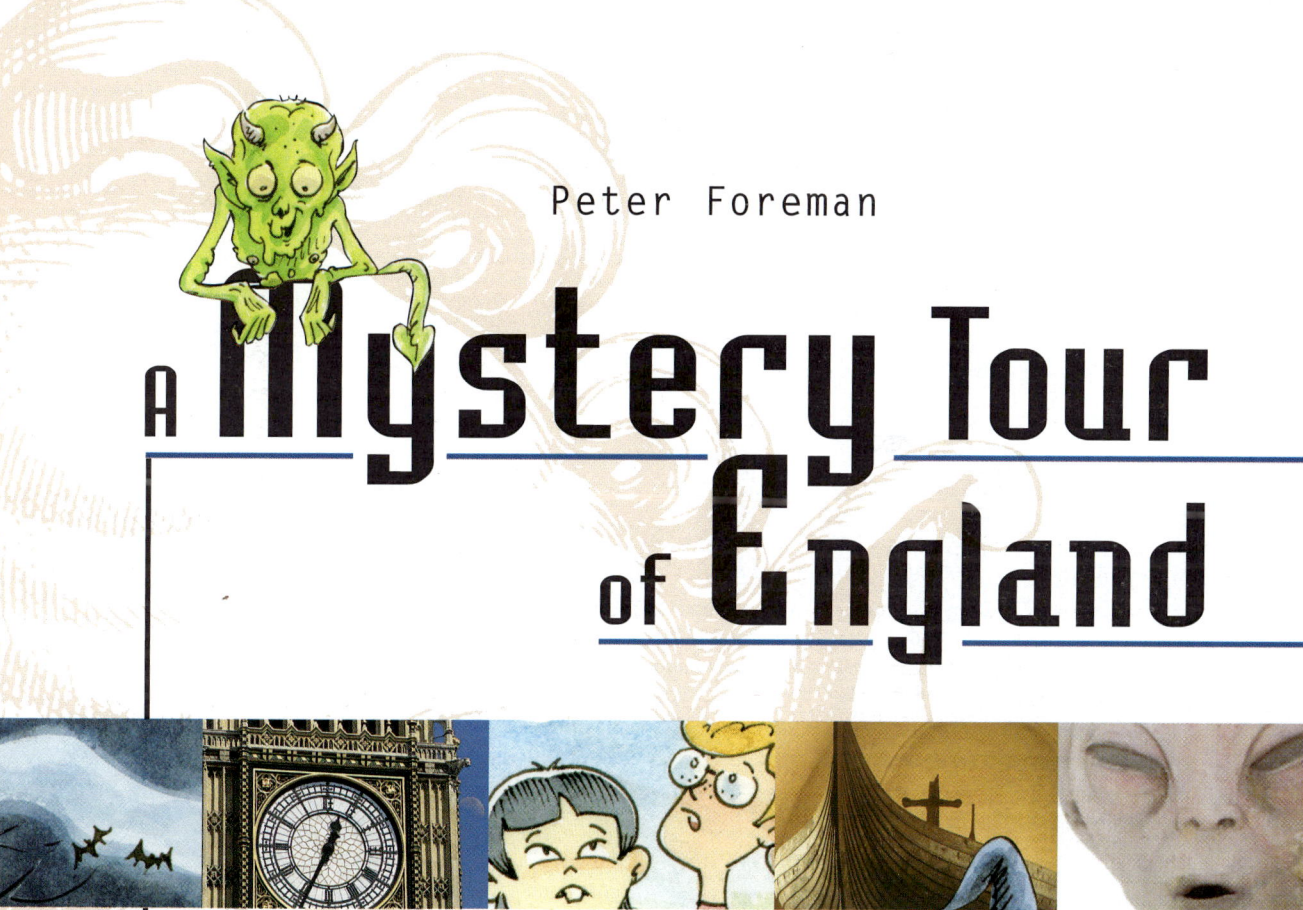

A Mystery Tour of England

Editors: Frances Evans, Monika Marszewska, Claudia Fiocco
Design: Nadia Maestri
Layout: Simona Corniola
Illustrations: Franco Grazioli
Photographs: Emilio Zanelli, Cideb archives

© 2001 Black Cat Publishing,
   an imprint of Cideb Editrice, Genoa, Canterbury

First edition: February 2001

10   9   8   7   6   5   4

Picture Credits

Abbreviations: f = far; b = bottom; c = centre; l = left; r = right; t = top.

By courtesy of the National Portrait Gallery, London: 41 tr *Sir Walter Raleigh* by Nicholas Hilliard (1547-1617); br *Rudyard Kipling* by Sir Philip Burne-Jones; 69 fbl *Charles Lutwidge Dodgson* (Pen name Lewis Carroll) by unknown photographer; 69 bl *Percy Bysshe Shelley* by Amelia Curran d. 1847; 71 bl *William Wordsworth* by Benjamin Robert Haydon; 71 bc *Samuel Taylor Coleridge* by Peter Vandyke (1729-99);71 br *George Gordon, 6th Baron Byron* (1835) by Thomas Phillips (1770-1845).

National Maritime Museum, Greenwich, London: 41 tl *Sir Francis Drake* by Gheeraerts M. 1561-1635 (style of).

By permission of the National Library of Australia: 41 bl *Portrait of Cook* (*c*. 1800) copy of Nathaniel Dance's portrait in the National Maritime Museum (UK).

Royal Shakespeare Theatre Collection, Stratford: 46b The 'Flower' Portrait of Shakespeare.

The author would like to thank Kevin Mulvany and Susan Rogers for the use of the photographs on pages 17 and 18.

Acknowledgements for all other material reproduced in this book can be found under the reproduction itself.

While every effort has been made to trace and acknowledge all copyright holders, we would like to apologise should there have been any errors or omissions.

All rights reserved. No part of this book may be reproduced, stored in a retrieval system, or transmitted, in any form or by any means, electronic, mechanical, photocopying, recording or otherwise, without the written permission of the publisher.

We would be happy to receive your comments and suggestions, and give you any other information concerning our material. Our e-mail and web-site addresses are:
info@blackcat-cideb.com
http://www.blackcat-cideb.com

ISBN 88-7754-619-0 Book + CD

Printed in Italy by Stige, Torino

INTRODUCTION

All aboard the coach for a mystery tour round England to practise your English!

In **A Mystery Tour of England** you are going on a trip to visit six cities, which you can follow on a map. Each city has a spooky mystery for you to discover, like UFOs or poltergeists, and you will also solve the mysteries of England's history, culture, and attractions, which include witches and Stonehenge.

A Mystery Tour combines practice, fun and mystery!

Each unit includes a **Mystery History** section and a **Timechart** to help you find out about English history. The **Pen and Ink Link** features famous English writers. And there is also a **Word Wizard**, who will help you revise your word-power with magic, and a **Grammar Ghoul** to guide you through the horrors of grammar!

There are a lot of exciting exercises and activities to make your trip interesting and freshen up your English.

At the back you will find a **revision test** for each unit. The teacher's book has an exit test and a student's portfolio.

A **CD** containing a variety of listening tasks is linked to your tour.

Have a spooky trip!

Peter Foreman

CONTENTS

MYSTERY STOP		HISTORY/MODERN TOPIC
MYSTERY STOP 1 Ghosts	7	The Romans
		British houses
Revision Test		
MYSTERY STOP 2 Close Encounters	21	Early and medieval Britain – Stonehenge
Revision Test		Religion in Britain
MYSTERY STOP 3 The *Titanic*	35	The Tudor and Stuart monarchies – the Empire
Revision Test		The Empire strikes back
MYSTERY STOP 4 Strange Happenings	49	The age of expansion – historical London
Revision Test		Time out in London
MYSTERY STOP 5 Psychic Experiences	63	The age of industrialism – witches/Oxford and Cambridge
Revision Test		Education in Britain
MYSTERY STOP 6 The Yorkshire Ripper	77	19th-century reform – the Industrial Revolution
Revision Test		British inventions

4 Complete the sentences with the words provided. Then match the places with the correct pictures.

> pub   borrow books   bank
> supermarket   send letters   are ill

You go to...

a. a hospital when you ………………………………………… .
b. a library to ………………………………………… .
c. a ………………………………………… to buy food.
d. a ………………………………………… when you need money.
e. a post office to ………………………………………… .
f. a ………………………………………… to drink beer.

5 Now write similar sentences about:

a. a restaurant …………………………………………………………
b. a bookshop …………………………………………………………
c. a cinema ……………………………………………………………

MYSTERY STOP 1

What is the name of the city? Read the clues and look at the map on page 6.

> It's in the south-west of Britain.
> You've got one in your house.

The city is called ....

1 You are going on a ghost walk around the city.
Listen (as many times as necessary) and match the ghosts with the places.
Write a, b, c etc. in the boxes.

a. The man with the black hat   1. ☐ a house
b. Juliana Popjoy   2. ☐ a street
c. Admiral Arthur Philip   3. ☐ a pub
d. The lady in grey   4. ☐ a restaurant

2 Now listen again and write the number of the ghost in the correct box on the map.

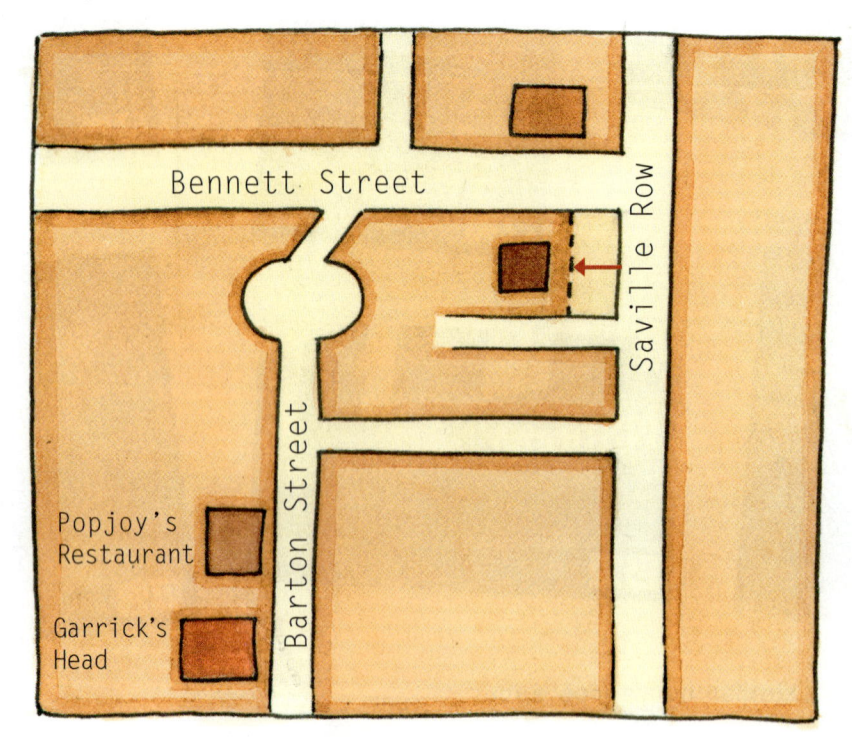

3 How much can you remember about the ghosts? Tell your partner about two of them. Your partner will tell you about the other two.

SCOTLAND
Atlantic Ocean
North Sea
Irish Sea
WALES
St. George's Channel
Cambridge
ENGLAND
London
Bath
Bristol Channel
Salisbury
Atlantic Ocean
English Channel
Southampton

GRAMMAR	LANGUAGE SKILLS	VOCABULARY
Present Simple – *do/does* Present Continuous – *be + -ing* Countable/uncountable nouns *Much, many, a lot of, a little, a few* Prepositions of place	Writing a letter Restaurant role-play Describing your home Interview Listening/identifying	Housing/public places Food
Past Simple Comparatives	Listening/identifying Describing people Writing a letter	Descriptive adjectives Religions Transport
Past Simple vs. Past Continuous Superlatives Question words Prepositions of time and movement *Like* (as preposition)	Listening/identifying Describing the lives of other people	Geography Nationalities Adjectives
Past Simple vs. Present Perfect Imperatives Singular/plural nouns	Using a brochure Listening/identifying Writing a short guide Using advertisements Writing a dialogue	British politics Occupations/ work places Verb opposites
Can/can't Past Simple Passive Short answers Articles	Listening/identifying Defining words Describing education systems Talking about favourite things	Categories Education Media
Will vs. *going to* *If* clauses (1st conditional) Possessive adjectives/pronouns	Describing people Listening/identifying Completing a map key Predicting the future	British sports and activities Inventions/discoveries Environmental issues

6 Strange things are happening in this haunted* house! First complete the sentences on page 10 with the correct Present Continuous form of the verbs provided. Sentence a has been done for you. Then match the sentences with the pictures in the house.

* See glossary at the end of the book.

1

> move ~~move~~ play strike go

Write your own sentence for f.

a. The curtains *are moving* in a room with a closed window.
b. A grandfather clock .... thirteen.
c. A ghost .... through the walls.
d. A ghost .... up the stairs.
e. Two hands .... the piano.
f. ....

7 You live in a haunted house. Write a letter to the editor of *The Supernatural* magazine describing what happens. Begin like this:

Dear Sir,
I think there is a ghost in my house.

Here are some ideas to help you: footsteps,* ghostly laughs, knocking on wall(s), very cold room(s), furniture moves, doors and windows open and close, ghostly figures appear and disappear.

Pen and Ink Link

Jane Austen's (1775-1817) family moved to Bath in 1801. She lived there for four years and wrote about it in some of her stories, like *Persuasion*. Her novels are mostly about social relationships, especially love and marriage. *Pride and Prejudice* and *Emma* are works of art. She was the first great English female novelist. There are many films and TV serials of her books.

Jane Austen by Cassandra Austen.
By courtesy of the
National Portrait Gallery, London.

8 Tick (✓) the correct answer.

Jane Austen:
a. ☐ wrote TV serials;
b. ☐ was born in Bath;
c. ☐ wrote about love and marriage.

Elizabeth and Darcy on their wedding day.
Pride and Prejudice (BBC).

Mystery History

9 In the year 43 AD the Romans invaded Britain. Read and listen to the letter from Flaminius, a Roman soldier, to his family and answer the questions.

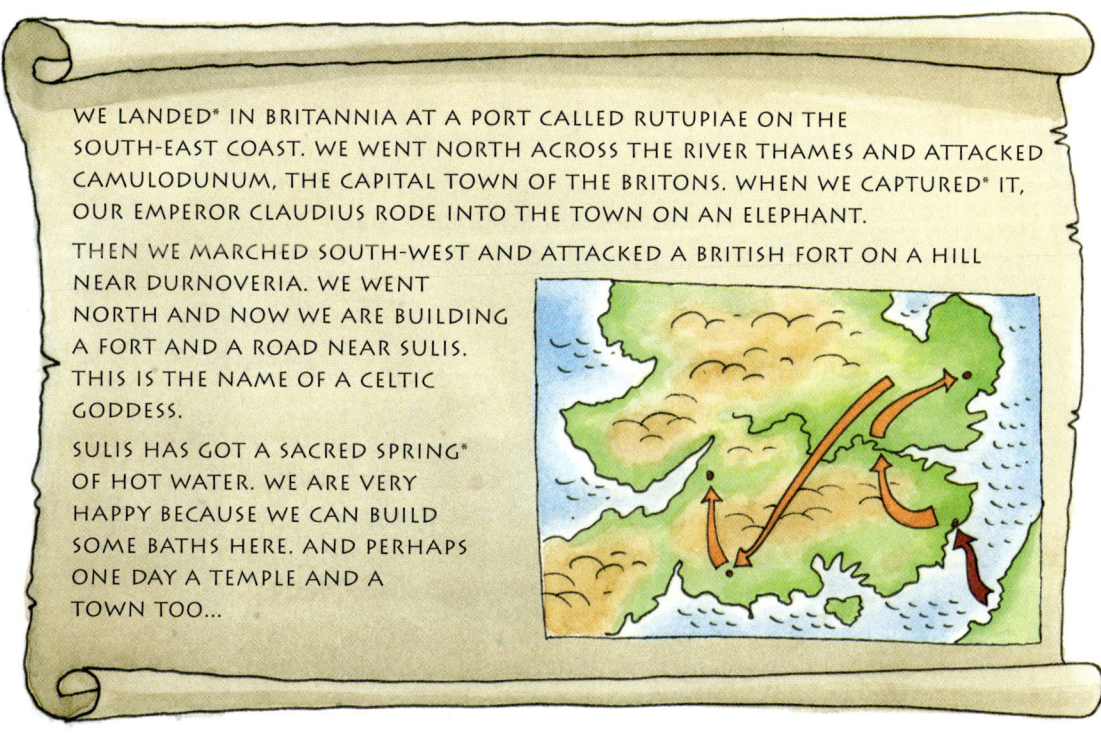

> WE LANDED* IN BRITANNIA AT A PORT CALLED RUTUPIAE ON THE SOUTH-EAST COAST. WE WENT NORTH ACROSS THE RIVER THAMES AND ATTACKED CAMULODUNUM, THE CAPITAL TOWN OF THE BRITONS. WHEN WE CAPTURED* IT, OUR EMPEROR CLAUDIUS RODE INTO THE TOWN ON AN ELEPHANT.
>
> THEN WE MARCHED SOUTH-WEST AND ATTACKED A BRITISH FORT ON A HILL NEAR DURNOVERIA. WE WENT NORTH AND NOW WE ARE BUILDING A FORT AND A ROAD NEAR SULIS. THIS IS THE NAME OF A CELTIC GODDESS.
>
> SULIS HAS GOT A SACRED SPRING* OF HOT WATER. WE ARE VERY HAPPY BECAUSE WE CAN BUILD SOME BATHS HERE. AND PERHAPS ONE DAY A TEMPLE AND A TOWN TOO...

First write the names of the towns on the map and then decide if the sentences are true (T) or false (F). Correct the false ones.

		T	F
a.	The Romans landed in the south-east of Britannia in 43 AD.	☐	☐
b.	They attacked the British capital north of the Thames.	☐	☐
c.	They didn't capture Camulodunum.	☐	☐
d.	The British fort was in the north-east.	☐	☐
e.	Flaminius was writing from Sulis.	☐	☐
f.	In 43 AD there was a town and baths at Sulis.	☐	☐

10 Use your answers to write a brief summary of Flaminius' letter.

11 Complete the sentences with the correct prepositions.

a. The Romans landed .... a port .... the south-east coast.
b. The Emperor Claudius rode .... an elephant.
c. The British fort was .... a hill .... Durnoveria.
d. There was a sacred spring of hot water .... Sulis.

12 The people of Britain were Celts. Their way of life was different from the Romans'. Look at the table and complete the text.

	huts*	towns	soap	good roads	gods	Latin	beer	vegetables	chariots*	fruit	Celtic
Romans		✓		✓	✓	✓		✓		✓	
Celts	✓		✓		✓		✓		✓		✓

The Romans built villas and houses, and they lived in ¹............... with streets and buildings. The Celts lived in small villages. They had round ²............... made of wood and straw.*
The Romans made the first good ³............... in Britain. The Roman soldiers rode horses or walked, but the Celts had fast ⁴............... . The Romans and the Celts had their ⁵............... and goddesses, like Minerva and Sulis. The ⁶............... spoke Celtic and the Romans ⁷............... . The Celts washed with ⁸............... ; the Romans used oil to clean themselves. The Celts usually drank ⁹............... .
They did not have a lot of fruit and vegetables. The ¹⁰............... brought carrots, peas, cabbage and other vegetables to Britain. They also introduced new kinds of ¹¹............... , like cherries, apples and grapes.

13 Listen to Flaminius talking about Celtic food. Then listen again and complete the table.

	not much	a few	a little	a lot of
eggs				
wine				
fruit	✓			
cereals				
fish				
vegetables				
milk				
meat				

14 Now use the table to complete the text. Listen again and check your answers.

The Celts eat only a ¹.................... vegetables and they haven't got ².................... fruit. They eat a ³.................... cereals, like oats, cooked with milk. But they don't drink ⁴.................... milk. Sometimes they eat a ⁵.................... meat, usually pork. They have a ⁶.................... fish, and there are a ⁷.................... eggs in their diet. They don't drink ⁸.................... wine because there aren't any grapes in Britannia. Generally, Celtic food is not very interesting.

TIMECHART

15 Read the timechart and complete the summary.

Roman Britain

AD
43	Emperor Claudius invades Britain.
c. 50	Foundation of Londinium.
61	Queen Boudicca leads* British rebellion. Defeated by Suetonius.
78	Agricola becomes governor.
122	Emperor Hadrian orders building of a wall across North Britain.
367	Barbarians attack Britain.
407	Roman army leaves Britain.
410	End of Roman rule* in Britain.

The Roman Province of Britannia

After Claudius' invasion, the Romans conquered Britain in about fifty years.
In ¹.................... the British tribes led by ².................... rebelled. They were defeated*. When Agricola became ³.................... in 78 AD, he built a palace at a commercial centre called Londinium.
Between 122-128 AD the Emperor ⁴.................... built a great ⁵.................... across the ⁶.................... of Britain.
Many ⁷.................... attacked Britain in 367 AD. When the Roman ⁸.................... left in 407 AD, the British could not defend themselves.

The tombstone of a Roman centurion called Marcus Favonius Facilis (1st century). Colchester Museums.

Hadrian's Wall as it stands today.

16 Flaminius is in a Roman restaurant in Britain. Read the menu and tick (✓) the photos that show the appropriate food. Use a dictionary if necessary.

Aquae Sulis Restaurant

First Course

Oysters*
Seagull* eggs in honey and pepper sauce
Snails* in milk

Main Course

Stuffed mice
Roast swan
Asparagus, peas, cabbage

Dessert

Panis dulcis (sweet bread)
Pastries filled with honey, nuts and raisins*
Selection of fruit (figs, cherries, grapes)

17 Flaminius is ordering a meal. The waiter's questions are in the correct order. Can you match them with Flaminius' answers?

WAITER

1. What would you like for the first course, sir?
2. I'm sorry, the oysters are finished. The snails are very good.
3. What about the main course?
4. Certainly, sir. And dessert?
5. No, sir. Only fruit.
6. Yes, sir. What would you like to drink?
7. Thank you, sir.

FLAMINIUS

a. Have you got any pastries?
b. Roast swan with asparagus.
c. I'd like some oysters, please.
d. All right, I'll have snails.
e. Red wine, please.
f. Well, bring me some figs.

1. ☐   4. ☐
2. ☐   5. ☐
3. ☐   6. ☐

18 Now YOU are in the restaurant. Use the menu on page 14 to write your own dialogue.
Or write a dialogue with your partner. One is the waiter, the other is the customer.

WAITER	CUSTOMER
....	....
....	....
....	....
....	....
....	....
....	....

Home Sweet Home

19 Look at the photos of homes on page 17. Which ones do the ghosts live in? First complete the ghosts' descriptions with the correct type of house. Then match them with the photos. Write a, b, c etc. in the boxes.

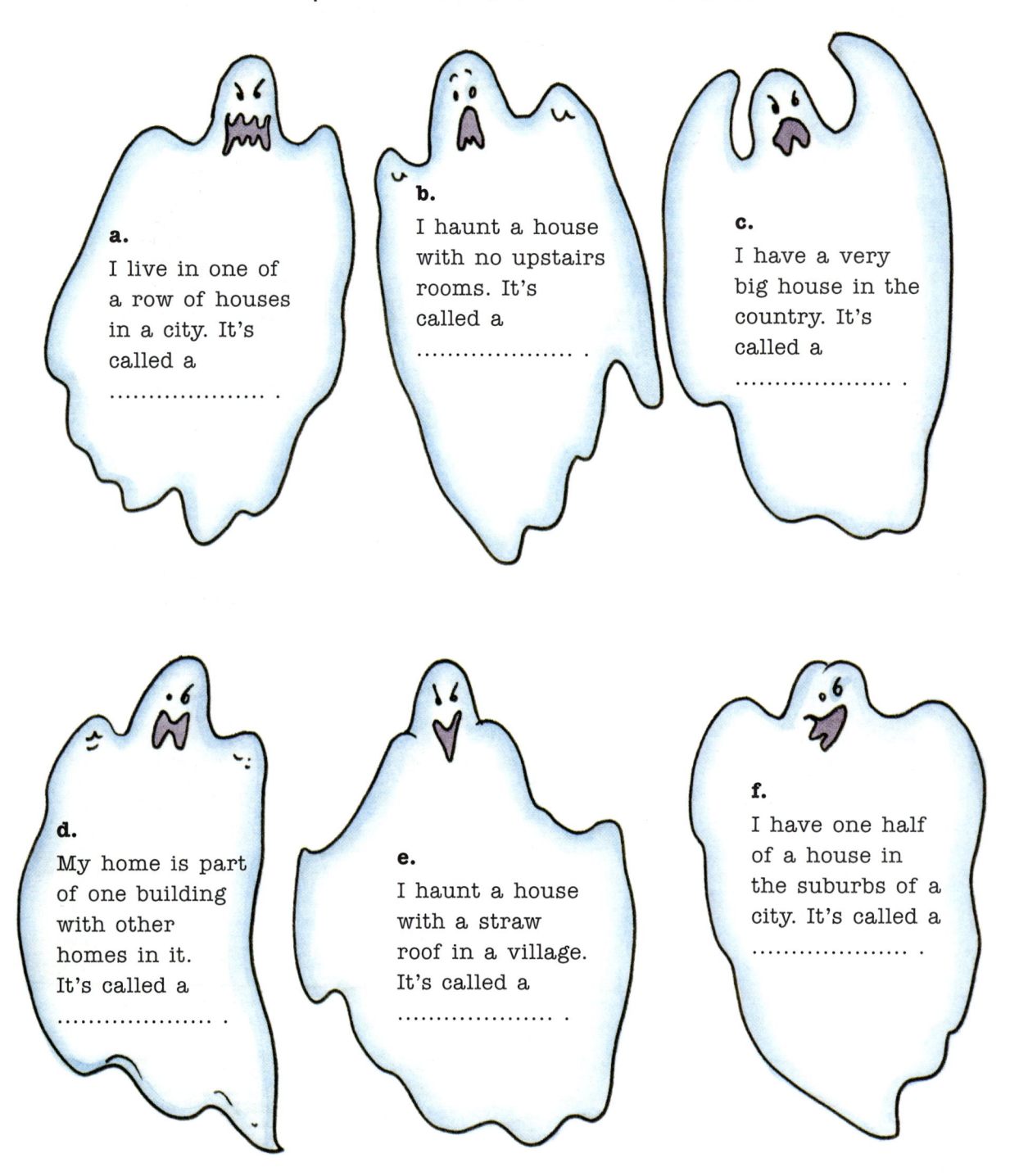

a. I live in one of a row of houses in a city. It's called a ....

b. I haunt a house with no upstairs rooms. It's called a ....

c. I have a very big house in the country. It's called a ....

d. My home is part of one building with other homes in it. It's called a ....

e. I haunt a house with a straw roof in a village. It's called a ....

f. I have one half of a house in the suburbs of a city. It's called a ....

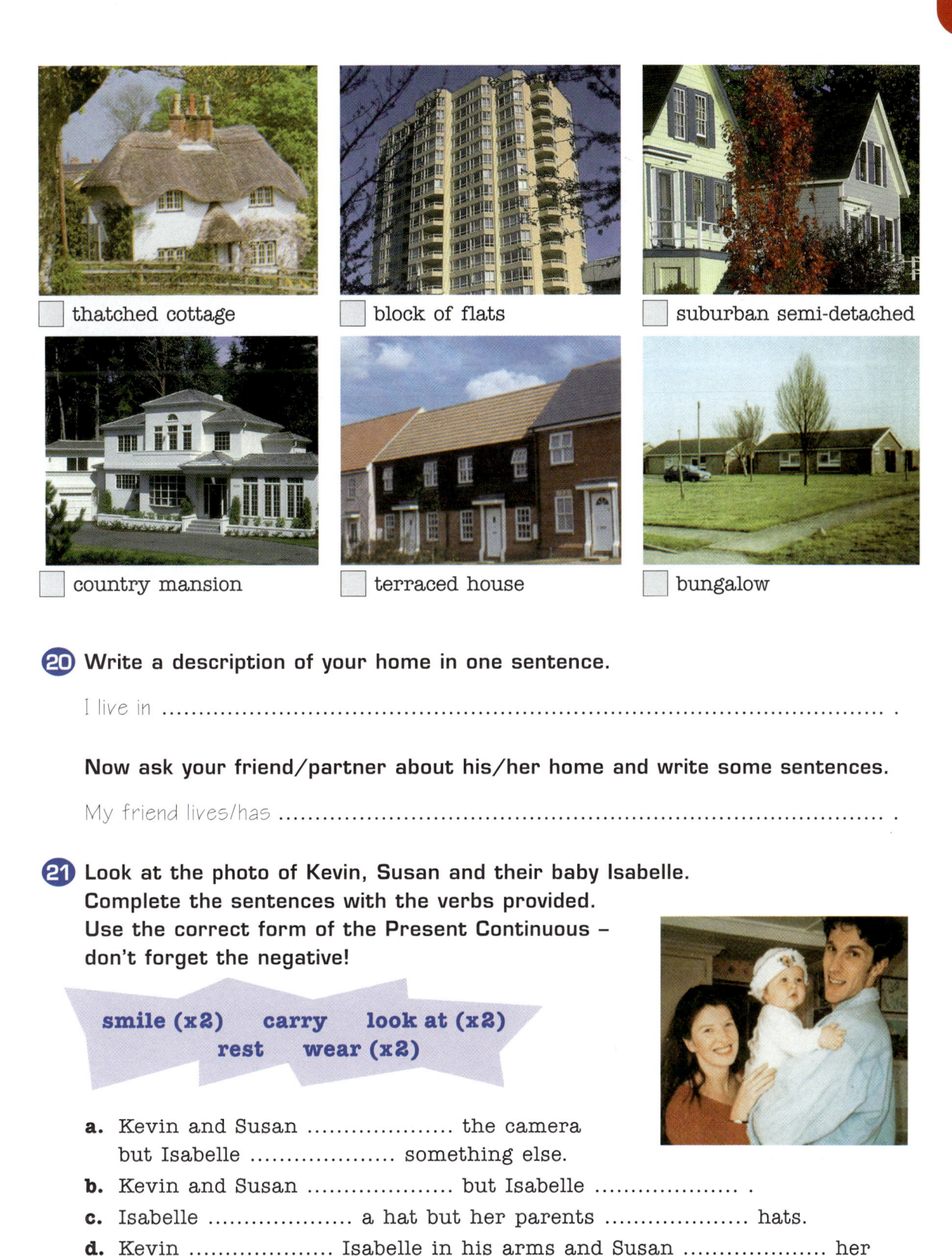

☐ thatched cottage   ☐ block of flats   ☐ suburban semi-detached

☐ country mansion   ☐ terraced house   ☐ bungalow

20 Write a description of your home in one sentence.

I live in ....

Now ask your friend/partner about his/her home and write some sentences.

My friend lives/has ....

21 Look at the photo of Kevin, Susan and their baby Isabelle.
Complete the sentences with the verbs provided.
Use the correct form of the Present Continuous –
don't forget the negative!

**smile (x2)   carry   look at (x2)
rest   wear (x2)**

a. Kevin and Susan .... the camera but Isabelle .... something else.
b. Kevin and Susan .... but Isabelle ....
c. Isabelle .... a hat but her parents .... hats.
d. Kevin .... Isabelle in his arms and Susan .... her hand on Kevin's arm.

22 Kevin and Susan have got an unusual job. Complete the interview with their answers in the bubbles.

> Fontainebleu, Versailles and Hampton Court Palace.
>
> Kevin makes the buildings and I paint and decorate them.
>
> We make mini-models of famous palaces, castles and country homes.
>
> American and Japanese museums.
>
> About a year.
>
> Buckingham Palace.

Interviewer: What do you and Susan do?
Kevin: ....
Interviewer: Give some examples, please, Susan.
Susan: ....
Interviewer: What famous building are you making now?
Kevin: ....
Interviewer: How long do you usually work on a model?
Kevin: ....
Interviewer: How do you and Kevin divide the work?
Susan: ....
Interviewer: Who buys your work?
Susan: ....

Can you continue the interview with your own questions?

The Word Wizard

23 The Word Wizard has a mixture of food in his cauldron. Unscramble the words to see what he's cooking.

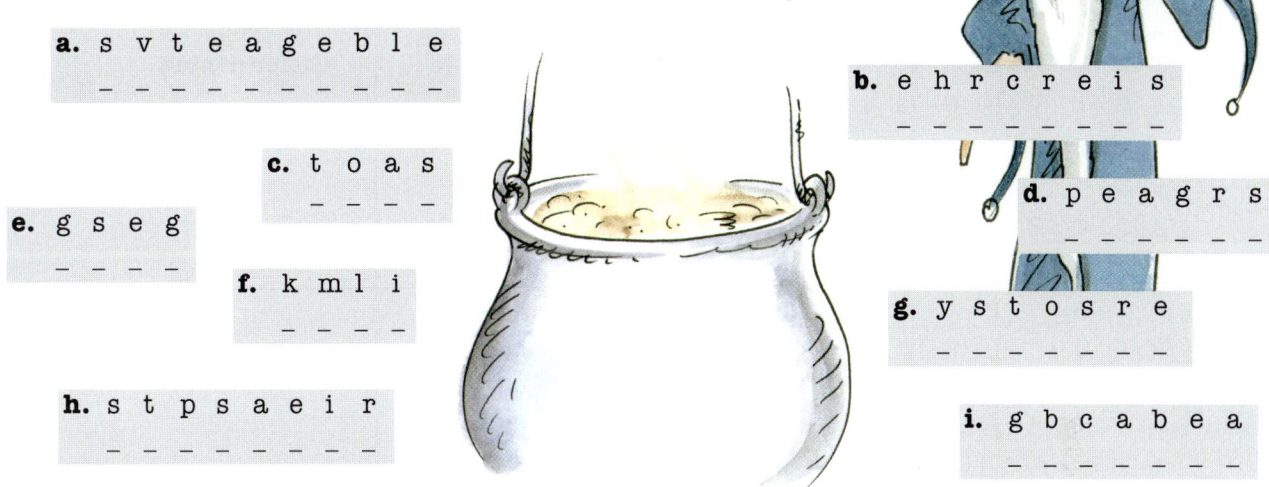

a. s v t e a g e b l e
_ _ _ _ _ _ _ _ _ _

b. e h r c r e i s
_ _ _ _ _ _ _ _

c. t o a s
_ _ _ _

d. p e a g r s
_ _ _ _ _ _

e. g s e g
_ _ _ _

f. k m l i
_ _ _ _

g. y s t o s r e
_ _ _ _ _ _ _

h. s t p s a e i r
_ _ _ _ _ _ _ _

i. g b c a b e a
_ _ _ _ _ _ _

24 The Wizard has broken these words in two with his magic. Can you find the two parts and put them back together? Write them in the correct part of the house.

cur

flo

do

wa

ro

sta

att

ic

irs

ll

of

tains

or

or

19

1

The Grammar Ghoul

25 The Grammar Ghoul likes old, bad food, like in the pictures. Find the food in the puzzle and complete the table.

```
S X M B R E A D V T
A B E T B G M L Z O
U I A C R I S P S M
S S T V W A T E R A
A C C H E E S E Y T
G U Q R O M G L C O
E I A P P L E J K U
K T M I L K Q E G G
P A S T A W Z Y B E
D A S C D G W I N E
```

Countable	Uncountable
biscuit	

26 Complete the Ghoul's questions with *Do/Does* or *Is/Are*. Then match them with the correct answer. Write a, b, c etc. in the boxes.

a. .... Juliana Popjoy walk around a restaurant?

b. .... Kevin and Susan make films?

c. .... the man in Saville Row wear modern clothes?

d. .... the ghost on page 9 moving through the walls?

e. .... Kevin and Susan making a model of Buckingham Palace?

f. .... two hands playing a guitar on page 9?

1. ☐ No, they don't.
2. ☐ Yes, it is.
3. ☐ Yes, they are.
4. ☐ Yes, she does.
5. ☐ No, they aren't.
6. ☐ No, he doesn't.

➡ Now turn to page 91 for the Revision Test.

Mystery Stop 2

Where is Warminster? Read the clues and look at the map on page 6.

> It's in the south of Britain.
> It's between Bath and Salisbury.

Write Warminster in the correct place on the map.

1 The Warminster Thing arrives. Listen and number the pictures in the correct order. Write 1, 2, 3 etc. in the boxes.

a ☐ b ☐ c ☐
d ☐ e ☐ f ☐

2 Complete the sentences with the past form of the verbs provided. Listen again to check your answers.

> fall   see   wake   be   grow   think

a. A strange noise .... postman Roger Rump.
b. 'I .... something was pulling tiles off the roof,' he said.
c. Housewife Rachel Attwell .... an object in the sky.
d. 'It .... like an enormous cigar,' she said.
e. Some pigeons .... from the sky.
f. Some flowers .... nearly four metres tall.

2

6 3 Read and listen to the newspaper article and tick (✔) the correct answers.

16th September 1976

THE WARMINSTER HERALD

TOURIST HAS CLOSE ENCOUNTER WITH THE WARMINSTER THING

German tourist Willy Gehlen believes he had a close encounter with the Warminster Thing. It happened late at night on September 14th.
'I was driving near the village of Upton Scudamore, two miles from Warminster,' Herr Gehlen said. 'I couldn't find a camping site* so I decided to stop near a farm gate and sleep in my car.'
At 3am he was woken by a humming* sound, like lots of bees, and then he saw a figure behind the gate.
'He was about two metres tall and he had a white face, big pink eyes and yellow hair,' said the tourist. 'His head was large and his ears were long. He wore silver clothes and luminous boots. There was a square torch on his belt.* It had a dark orange light and he shone* it at me.'
Herr Gehlen said he wasn't frightened because he thought it was a farmer. He started to make some coffee but when he looked again the man wasn't there.
'I heard the humming sound again and saw a large thing going up into the sky. Then I realised* it was a close encounter of the third

a. Willy Gehlen was
1. ☐ a farmer;
2. ☐ British;
3. ☐ on holiday.

b. The encounter happened
1. ☐ on a camping site;
2. ☐ not far from Warminster;
3. ☐ in a car.

c. Gehlen was woken by
1. ☐ some bees;
2. ☐ a sound;
3. ☐ a stranger.

d. The figure had
1. ☐ yellow ears and pink hair;
2. ☐ white hair and yellow eyes;
3. ☐ pink eyes and long ears.

e. The figure
1. ☐ had dark clothes;
2. ☐ shone a light at Gehlen;
3. ☐ had an orange on his belt.

f. Gehlen thought the figure was
1. ☐ probably a farmer;
2. ☐ not very tall;
3. ☐ frightened.

g. When he saw the moving object he realised he'd had a close encounter of the
1. ☐ third kind;
2. ☐ second kind;
3. ☐ first kind.

4 Read the reporter's questions about another alien encounter and write the witness' answers in the spaces using the sentences in the box below. Then tick (✔) the picture that matches the description of the alien.

Reporter: How tall was the alien?
Witness: ....
Reporter: Was it big?
Witness: ....
Reporter: What about its head? Was it large or small?
Witness: ....
Reporter: Can you describe its eyes?
Witness: ....
Reporter: Did it have any hair?
Witness: ....
Reporter: What was it wearing?
Witness: ....

> They were round and green.
> It had white, luminous clothes.
> Quite large, like a football.
> No, it was small and thin.
> Not very tall. About 1m.
> No, it was bald.

a ☐   b ☐   c ☐

5 Choose *one* of the other two pictures and describe the alien.

6 Write a letter to your friend describing a close encounter that YOU had with an alien.

2

Mystery History

Stonehenge, an ancient monument on Salisbury Plain, is one of the great mysteries of Britain.

Read the information and answer questions 7 and 8 on page 26.

FACTS

- Stonehenge is as old as the pyramids of Egypt.
- Work began about 2800 BC and ended about 1500 BC.
- It is orientated to the midsummer sunrise* (June 21st) and the midwinter sunrise (December 21st).
- Some stones came from South Wales, 400 kilometres away.

THEORIES

Stonehenge was:
- built by the Romans;
- a memorial* to British warriors* killed by Saxons;
- built by Merlin the Magician;
- used for human sacrifice by Celtic priests called Druids;
- an energy transmitter for UFOs;
- an observatory or calendar for calculating astronomical events.

MYSTERIES

- How did primitive people build it?
- Why did they build it in that particular place?
- Why did they suddenly stop work and abandon it?
- How did they understand the mathematics of Pythagoras and Euclid before the Greeks?
- Why didn't the engineers invent the wheel* to help them transport the stones?

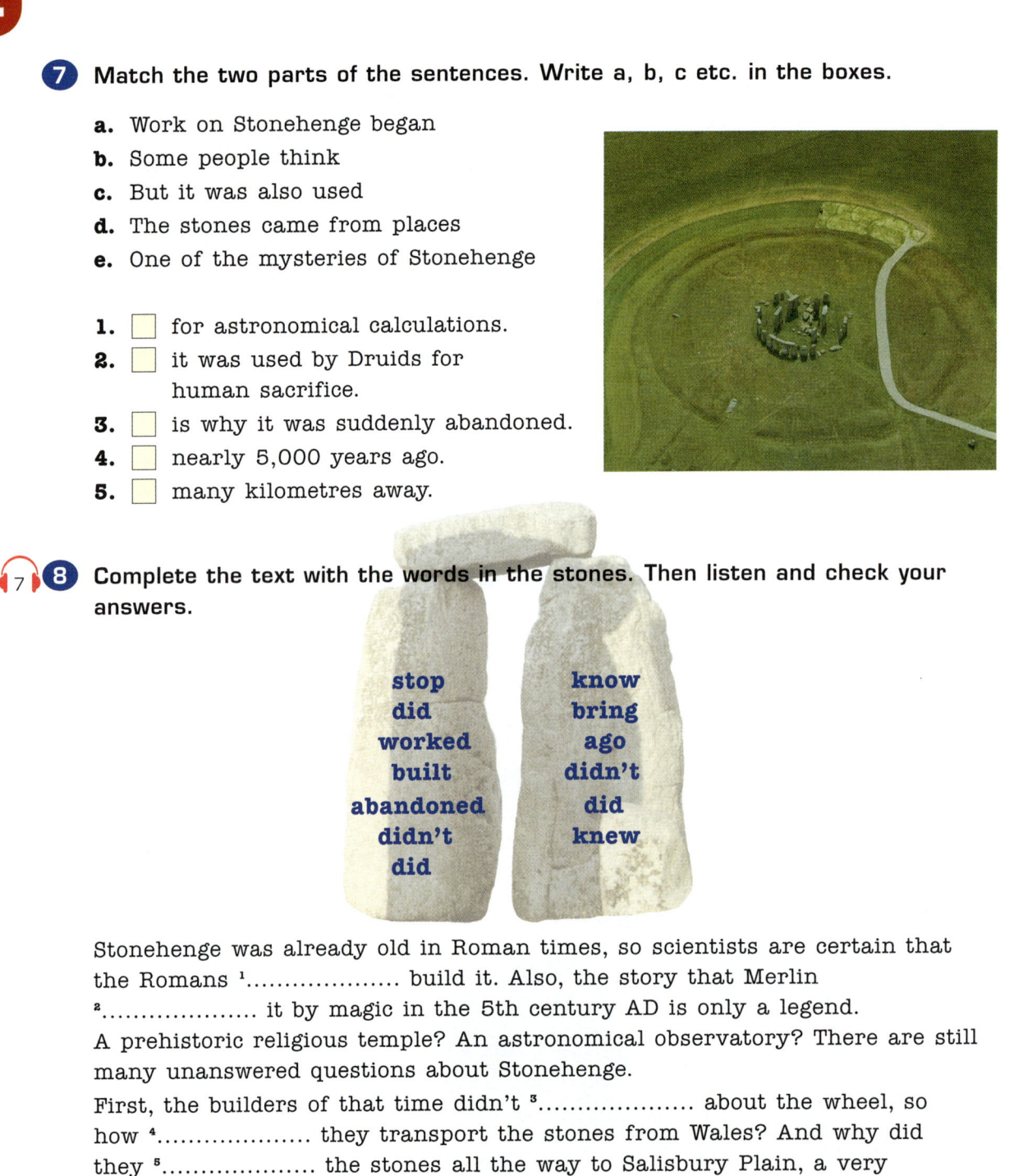

7 Match the two parts of the sentences. Write a, b, c etc. in the boxes.

a. Work on Stonehenge began
b. Some people think
c. But it was also used
d. The stones came from places
e. One of the mysteries of Stonehenge

1. ☐ for astronomical calculations.
2. ☐ it was used by Druids for human sacrifice.
3. ☐ is why it was suddenly abandoned.
4. ☐ nearly 5,000 years ago.
5. ☐ many kilometres away.

8 Complete the text with the words in the stones. Then listen and check your answers.

stop
did
worked
built
abandoned
didn't
did

know
bring
ago
didn't
did
knew

Stonehenge was already old in Roman times, so scientists are certain that the Romans ¹.................... build it. Also, the story that Merlin ².................... it by magic in the 5th century AD is only a legend.
A prehistoric religious temple? An astronomical observatory? There are still many unanswered questions about Stonehenge.
First, the builders of that time didn't ³.................... about the wheel, so how ⁴.................... they transport the stones from Wales? And why did they ⁵.................... the stones all the way to Salisbury Plain, a very difficult journey? Secondly, the builders ⁶.................... about Greek mathematics before the Greeks! How ⁷.................... ancient Britons possess this knowledge 4,800 years ⁸.................... ?
But perhaps the biggest mystery is why the builders ⁹.................... Stonehenge. They ¹⁰.................... on it for 1,300 years. So why ¹¹.................... they continue? Why ¹².................... they ¹³.................... so suddenly?

9 Can you make questions from these statements?

    a. The builders began work on Stonehenge about 2800 BC.
When .... ?

    b. Some stones came from Wales.
Where .... ?

    c. The builders built Stonehenge on Salisbury Plain.
Where .... ?

    d. They understood Greek mathematics.
What .... ?

    e. We don't know why they stopped work suddenly.
Why .... ?

TIMECHART

10 Read the timechart and match three dates with the pictures.

Early and Medieval Britain

AD
- 435-550   The Anglo-Saxon invasions.
- 790   The Vikings begin to attack Britain.
- 878   King Alfred defeats the Danes.
- 1066   The Norman invasion.
- 1215   King John signs* the Magna Carta. Beginning of political freedom.
- 1295   The first parliament of Edward I. Beginning of democracy.
- 1455-85   The Wars of the Roses between the noble families of York and Lancaster. The wars end with the death of Richard III at the Battle of Bosworth.

Magna Carta.
By permission of the British Library.

The *Bayeux Tapestry* narrates events leading up to the Norman invasion of England.
Bayeux Tapestry 11th century. By special permission of the city of Bayeux.

A Viking ship similar to those used to attack Britain.
Vikingskipsmuseet, Oslo.

a. .... AD   **b.** .... AD   **c.** .... AD

11 Salisbury was built about 770 years ago near Stonehenge. It was a medieval new town. But why was it built? Read the letter from Bishop Poore to Henry III, who was 13 years old.

> Old Sarum, February 1220
>
> Your Royal Majesty,
>
> My dream is to build a beautiful cathedral in a new town called Salisbury. So we must abandon Old Sarum. It is an old town and now it is too small. It is cold because it is situated on a high, rocky hill, and there isn't much water.
>
> The site of the new town will be in the valley by the River Avon. It is flat, green and warm – with plenty of water.
>
> The cathedral will be built in a new style of architecture. With modern techniques we can build it in a short time. It will be a miracle and many visitors will come to see it. The new town will bring money and prosperity!
>
> Regards,
> Bishop Poore

12 Now match the two parts of the sentences. Write a, b, c etc. in the boxes.

a. Bishop Poore wants to build a new cathedral
b. He decides to move the old town of Old Sarum
c. The new town of Salisbury will
d. The cathedral will be built
e. The bishop believes his idea

1. ☐ be by the River Avon.
2. ☐ to a better site.
3. ☐ in a new town.
4. ☐ will attract visitors.
5. ☐ in a new style with modern techniques.

The ruins of the original town, Bishop's Palace and Norman castle, together with the foundations of the cathedral of Old Sarum can still be seen on high ground north of Salisbury.

Salisbury from the Ramparts of Old Sarum by J. M. W. Turner.
© Salisbury & South Wiltshire Museum.

13 Complete the text with the adjectives provided.

> flat   old   high   short   modern   warm   small
> beautiful   green   new   rocky   cold

THE MIRACLE OF SALISBURY CATHEDRAL

Bishop Poore decided to abandon Old Sarum because it was [1].................... and too [2].................... . Its site on a [3]...................., [4].................... hill meant that it was [5].................... and there wasn't much water. So he wanted to build a [6].................... cathedral in the valley by the River Avon, where it was [7]...................., [8].................... , and [9].................... . Work began in April 1220 and the cathedral was finished in 1258. This is a very [10].................... period of time. The cathedral was built in a [11].................... style of Gothic architecture, using [12].................... techniques.

14 Read this true story about a medieval crime and find a correct answer to the seven questions on page 30 (there are too many answers!) Write a, b, c etc. in the boxes.

MURDER IN THE CATHEDRAL

In December 1170 King Henry II was very angry with his friend Thomas Becket, the Archbishop of Canterbury, because Becket said the church was more important than the king. Henry said some angry words: 'Who will do something about this priest?'

What did Henry mean? Four of his soldiers thought he meant: 'Who will go and kill Becket?' So they went to Canterbury Cathedral and killed him. The murder shocked all Europe. Becket became a saint in 1173. Millions of pilgrims visited his tomb in the cathedral.

2

a. Was Becket angry with Henry II?
b. Were Becket and the king enemies*?
c. Did Becket think the king was greater than the church?
d. Did the soldiers think Henry wanted them to kill Becket?
e. Did the murder happen in 1173?
f. Was Becket killed in Canterbury Cathedral?
g. Did Becket become a saint?

Canterbury Cathedral.

1. ☐ Yes, they did.   2. ☐ No, they didn't.   3. ☐ No, they weren't.
4. ☐ Yes, they were. 5. ☐ No, it didn't.   6. ☐ No, he didn't.
7. ☐ Yes, he was.   8. ☐ Yes, he did.   9. ☐ No, he wasn't.

15 In your opinion, did Henry want the soldiers to kill Becket? Complete one answer and say why.

Yes, ...
No, ...

Pen and Ink Link

16 Read the text and answer the question.

Geoffrey Chaucer (c. 1343-1400) wrote *The Canterbury Tales* in a London dialect called Middle English. Many poets wrote in Latin, so Chaucer is called the Father of English Literature. In his famous work some pilgrims who are going to Becket's tomb in Canterbury decide to tell stories on the way. There is a knight, the wife of Bath (married five times!) and men and women of the Church. Chaucer created a picture of medieval English society.

Geoffrey Chaucer copy by unknown artist, after unknown artist.
By courtesy of the National Portrait Gallery, London.

The pilgrims outside the walls of the city of Canterbury by John Lydgate (1370?-1449).
By permission of the British Library.

Why is Chaucer called the Father of English Literature?

Religion in Britain

17 Listen and tick (✔) the correct answers.

a. The official religion is
  1. ☐ Greek Orthodox
  2. ☐ Protestant Christianity
  3. ☐ Catholic Christianity

b. Who is the Head of the Church?
  1. ☐ The Prime Minister
  2. ☐ Prince Charles
  3. ☐ The Queen

c. The total number of Hindus and Sikhs is about
  1. ☐ 6,000,000
  2. ☐ 60,000
  3. ☐ 600,000

d. About 350,000 people are
  1. ☐ Buddhist
  2. ☐ Jewish
  3. ☐ Muslim

18 Match the bubbles on the right with the correct photo, like the example. Then write the religions below each picture.

Buddhism   Islam   Rastafarianism   Hindu

1 Jamal
I was born 12 years ago in Pakistan, but I live in Birmingham. I'm a Muslim.

a ☐
My family are Rastafarians. It's a way of life like Christianity. It started in Jamaica in the 1920s.

....

2 Shanti
I'm 8 years old. I was born in India and am a Hindu, but I live in East London.

b ☐
We believe in one God called Allah. Our prophet is Mohammed, who lived many years ago.

....

3 Vidhisha
I'm 10. I was born in Ilford, England, but my parents came from Sri Lanka. We are Buddhists.

c 3
We follow a great teacher called the Buddha. He taught in the 6th century BC.

....

4 Tobias
I was born in Brixton, London, in 1985. My parents came from Jamaica.

d ☐
My religion began 4,500 years ago in India. We have many gods. The most important is Brahman.

....

19 Now answer the questions with complete sentences.

a. When did the Hindu religion begin?
   It ....
b. When was Tobias born?
   ....
c. When did the Buddha teach?
   ....
d. When did the prophet Mohammed live?
   ....

20 Write questions for these answers.

a. .... 12 years ago.
b. .... In the 1920s.

21 Can you remember what famous events happened on these dates?
Write the correct name/place and verb (in the past form!) in the spaces.

Britain
Lady Diana
Cardinal Wojtyla
President Kennedy
John Lennon
the first men
Italy

win
(be) murdered
(be) assassinated
die   join
become   land

a. On November 22nd, 1963 .... in Dallas.
b. In July, 1969 .... on the moon.
c. In 1973 .... the European Economic Community.
d. On October 15th, 1979 .... Pope John Paul II.
e. In December, 1980 .... in New York.
f. In 1982 .... the World Cup.
g. On August 31st, 1997 .... in a car accident.

22 Can you explain the difference between 'murdered' and 'assassinated'? Use a dictionary to help you.

The Word Wizard

23 The Word Wizard has conjured up* the opposites of the adjectives in the table! Complete the table and the Wizard's description of himself.

big	
	short
square	
	dark
young	
	hot
long	
	low
black	
	old
fat	

round
high cold
small
light
white tall
thin old
short
new

I am the Word Wizard. I am ………. (about 1.90 m) and thin. I've got ………. eyes and a ………. nose. My hair is ………. and ………., like my beard. I wear a tall, ………. hat, and my coat is long and ………. . My magic is strong. Abracadabra!!!

24 Can you do the transport puzzle on the Wizard's balloon?

ACROSS
- **3** It's round and full of gas.
- **5** It's an animal with four legs.
- **7** It's got two wings.
- **8** It's got a propeller* on top of it.
- **11** It's got two wheels.

DOWN
- **1** You use it on a river or the sea.
- **2** You travel on it in the city.
- **4** It travels on the sea and it's bigger than 1 down.
- **6** Indians and Eskimos use it.
- **9** It's got four wheels.
- **10** It's got long carriages* and stops at stations.

25 Now put your answers in the correct column in the table.

Land	Sea	Air

The Grammar Ghoul

26 The Grammar Ghoul is going to bury the past verbs but he doesn't know which verbs are regular (-ed) or irregular. Can you help him? Put the verbs in their past form into the correct coffin.

look continue happen shine begin start want have put live write wear see kill hear build help come go make visit watch decide listen finish think paint

PAST IRREGULAR

PAST (-ED)

27 The Grammar Ghoul is dreaming of this exercise. Can you do it before he wakes up and the dream goes? Complete the sentences with the comparative (-er) form of the words provided.

fast   small   great   young   tall   old

a. Stonehenge was built 4,000 years ago. It is .... than Salisbury Cathedral.
b. The two-metre alien was .... than a man.
c. Shanti is 8 years old and Tobias is 15. Shanti is .... than Tobias.
d. A spaceship travels .... than a car.
e. Warminster is a town and Salisbury is a city. Warminster is .... than Salisbury.
f. Becket said the Church was .... than the king.

➡ Now turn to page 92 for the Revision Test.

Mystery Stop 3

Read the clue and look at the map on page 6.

> From Salisbury go south-east to the coast.

Complete the name of the port with the missing vowels.   S _ _ th _ mpt _ n

1 Read and listen to the review of a real novel by Morgan Robertson, published in 1898, and the newspaper report. Then complete the table.

BOOK REVIEW

AN UNBELIEVABLE STORY

June, 1898

This novel describes the first or maiden voyage of a transatlantic ship named *Titan*. The ship is 800 feet long, weighs 75,000 tons, and has three enormous propellers.
It is the largest and safest* ship in the world, and the owners say it is unsinkable*.
It leaves the port of Southampton in April on its first voyage to New York. It is carrying 3,000 passengers and crew*.
One cold night, travelling at a speed of 25 knots*, it hits* an iceberg in the middle of the Atlantic and sinks. Most of the passengers are lost because the *Titan* has only 24 lifeboats*!
This story is unbelievable!

MORGAN ROBERTSON
THE WRECK OF THE TITAN
A NINETEENTH-CENTURY PROPHECY

Fourteen years later *The New York Times* announced the tragedy of the *Titanic*.

Tuesday, April 16th, 1912

The New York Times

Titanic sinks four hours after hitting iceberg. 866 rescued, probably 1,250 lost.

The owners said it was unsinkable. The 66,000 ton White Star liner was the largest in the world. It was 882.5 feet long and had three huge* propellers. The *Titanic* left Southampton on April 10th for New York. It was carrying 2,207 passengers and crew – but only 20 lifeboats! On the third night it hit a large iceberg at a speed of 23 knots and sank four hours later. It was the *Titanic*'s maiden voyage.

	Fiction	Fact
Name of ship	....	Titanic
Voyage	....	maiden
Year of disaster	1898	....
Month of disaster	....	....
Port of embarkation	....	....
Destination	....	....
Passengers and crew	....	....
Lifeboats	....	....
Tonnage	75,000 tons	....
Length	....	....
Propellers	....	....
Cause of sinking	....	....
Speed at impact	....	....

2 Complete the sentences with the correct past form (continuous or simple) of the verbs in brackets.

a. The *Titanic* .... (*go*) to New York when it hit an iceberg.
b. The disaster .... (*happen*) when the *Titanic* was sailing in the North Atlantic.
c. When it hit the iceberg, the *Titanic* .... (*travel*) at a speed of 23 knots.
d. The *Titanic* was carrying 2,207 people when it .... (*leave*) Southampton.
e. Some passengers .... (*sleep*) when the ship hit the iceberg.

3 Write your own sentence using these key words.

The ship's orchestra/play/music/when/the *Titanic*/sink.
....

4 Now write questions, like the example.

a. What *were some passengers doing when the Titanic hit the iceberg* ?
b. Where .... ?
c. How fast .... ?
d. How many .... ?

5 Complete the text with the superlative form of the adjectives.

safe   long   sad   large   fast

Perhaps the most famous ship in the world is the *Titanic*. At 66,000 tons it was the ¹.................... transatlantic liner of the time. And it was also the ².................... – over 800 feet. With three huge propellers its ³.................... speed was 24 knots. The owners said it was the ⁴.................... ship in the world – in fact, they thought it was unsinkable. They were wrong! Three days after it sailed from Southampton it hit an iceberg in the North Atlantic and sank. Hundreds of lives were lost in the ⁵.................... tragedy in marine history.

Titanic in White Dock, by G. Fraser.

6 Read and listen to the story and complete the reporter's questions with the words provided. Then match the questions to their answers.

PRINCESS OF DEATH

Cairo, Egypt, 1910.

Douglas Murray, a British Egyptologist, bought the mummy-case* of an ancient Egyptian princess from an American. That evening the American died.

Later, Murray learnt that the princess had been a priestess* in the Cult of the Dead at the temple of Ammon-Ra in Thebes about 1600 BC. Writing on the walls of her tomb said terrible things would happen to anybody who disturbed her. Three days later on a shooting* expedition Murray's gun exploded in his hand. His arm was amputated in hospital.

Then, on the return voyage to England, two of Murray's friends died of mysterious causes. In London Murray decided to sell the mummy-case, but a woman friend asked him to give it to her. Soon the woman's mother died, her lover abandoned her, and she became very ill. After she returned the case to Murray, he gave it to the British Museum. A photographer was taking pictures of it when he suddenly fell down dead.

The British Museum offered the mummy-case to a museum in New York. The Americans asked the museum to send it by the safest way possible. So it was put on a new ship, the *Titanic*, making its maiden voyage on 10th April, 1912 from Southampton to New York. The mummy-case never arrived…

Who   What   Why   Where   How

REPORTER

a. .... did you buy the mummy-case?
b. .... sold it to you?
c. .... did you lose your arm?
d. .... did your woman friend return the case to you?
e. .... happened to the photographer in the British Museum?

MURRAY

1. ☐ My gun exploded in my hand.
2. ☐ In Cairo.
3. ☐ He fell down dead.
4. ☐ Because horrible things happened to her.
5. ☐ An American.

Mystery History

7 Read the information and answer the questions. Then write the name of the port on the map.

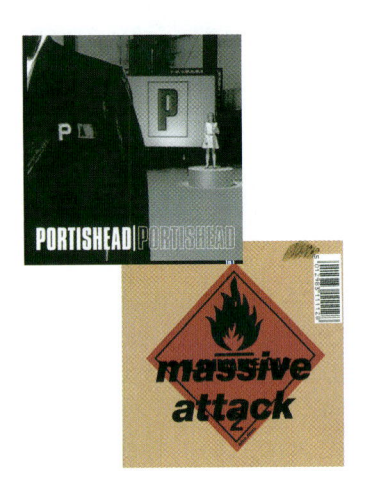

Bristol is on the south-west coast near Wales. In the 18th century it was a rich port which traded* in rum, tobacco, sugar and slaves*. Today it is the centre of the Bristol Sound, with bands like Massive Attack and Portishead.

a. What does the Bristol Sound refer to?

....

Whitby is a fishing port on the north-east coast of Yorkshire. In a famous horror story a ship arrives here with a strange passenger. He changes into a dog and escapes from the ship.

b. What is the name of the passenger?

....

Liverpool is in the north-west. In the 19th century it was the main port for European emigration. Nine million people emigrated between 1830-1930.

c. Which country did they go to?

....

38

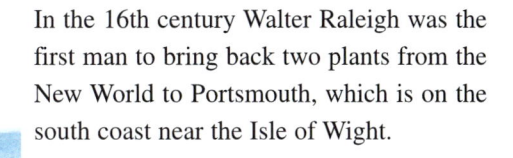

In the 16th century Walter Raleigh was the first man to bring back two plants from the New World to Portsmouth, which is on the south coast near the Isle of Wight.

d. What are the two plants called?

....

This famous character is in a story by Daniel Defoe. He sailed from Hull on the north-east coast and he was shipwrecked* on an island.

e. What is the name of the character?

....

In 1620 The Pilgrim Fathers sailed from Plymouth in south-west England to North America in the *Mayflower*. They founded* the colony of New Plymouth.

f. What ocean did the *Mayflower* cross?

....

39

8 Use the information in the box to complete the text.

Bristol
- slaves
- West Indian rum, tobacco, sugar
- England's second largest city

Liverpool
- transatlantic emigration
- first multi-ethnic city

Portsmouth
- Nelson's *Victory*

Plymouth
- Cook's three voyages of discovery
- Spanish Armada
- prison ships to Australia

London
- Indian silk, spices, tea
- American cotton, tobacco
- Canadian minerals, furs*

THE PORTS OF THE EMPIRE

In 1588 English ships sailed from [1].................... to attack the Spanish Armada. Two hundred years later Captain Cook's three great [2].................... started from the same port. And in the 19th century [3].................... transported prisoners from Plymouth to [4].................... . From [5].................... Admiral Nelson's ship *Victory* left to fight Napoleon's ships at Trafalgar in 1805. After London, [6].................... was the largest city in England. It became rich from the [7].................... trade, transporting Africans to the West Indies. Imports from the Caribbean included rum, tobacco and [8].................... . But the greatest port of the Empire was London. It imported tea and spices from [9].................... , tobacco and cotton from [10].................... and furs from [11].................... . The main port for transatlantic emigration was [12].................... , which became England's first [13].................... city.

Launch of Fireships Against the Armada by Netherlandish school, 16th century.
National Maritime Museum, Greenwich, London.

9 **Listen and match the people with the correct countries.**

1. Sir Francis Drake
2. Sir Walter Raleigh
3. Captain Cook
4. Rudyard Kipling

a.
b.
c.
d.

10 **Can you complete the sentences with the correct country or nation?**

   a. Drake went to .... to find slaves.
   b. Raleigh founded the North .... colony of Virginia.
   c. Cook's voyages helped the British to colonise ....
      and ....
   d. Kipling was born in ....

TIMECHART

11 Use the pictures below to complete the timechart.

The Tudor and Stuart Monarchies

AD
1485 — Henry VII begins Tudor dynasty.
1509 — Henry VIII's coronation.
1534-5 — Henry becomes Head of the Church of England.
1555 — Persecution of Protestants by Queen Mary I.
....
1603 — James I becomes the first Stuart king.
....
1642 — English Civil War begins.
....
1653 — Oliver Cromwell becomes Lord Protector.
1660 — The monarchy restored. Charles II becomes king.

Charles I by Daniel Mytens (1590-1648?).
By courtesy of the National Portrait Gallery, London.
Charles I was executed in 1649.

The Gunpowder Plotters, who in an act of Roman Catholic rebellion attempted to blow up* the Houses of Parliament on 5 November 1605.

Elizabeth I when Princess by unknown artist.
The Royal Collection © 2000, Her Majesty Queen Elizabeth II.
Elizabeth I (1558-1603).

12 Complete the sentences with some of the prepositions from page 43.

a. The *Mayflower* sailed .... the Atlantic in 65 days.
b. Robinson Crusoe climbed* .... a hill to get a good view of the island.
c. Dracula changed into a dog and jumped .... the ship.
d. The *Titanic* was going .... Southampton .... New York.
e. Robinson Crusoe was walking .... the beach when he saw a human footprint.*

f. The iceberg was coming slowly .... our ship.
g. The passengers panicked and jumped .... the sea.
h. The shipwrecked sailor was thrown .... a beach during a storm.

onto off across along

up down to from

into out of towards away from

13 Can you do this quick quiz from memory? Check your answers on pages 38-39.

a. Whitby is a port in the
  1. ☐ south-east
  2. ☐ north-east
  3. ☐ south-west

b. It's a port in the south-west.
  1. ☐ Liverpool
  2. ☐ Plymouth
  3. ☐ London

c. Bristol is on the
  1. ☐ north-west coast
  2. ☐ south coast
  3. ☐ south-west coast

d. It's a port in the south.
  1. ☐ Portsmouth
  2. ☐ Liverpool
  3. ☐ Hull

14 Do you know where these ports are located?

a. Sydney ....
b. Naples ....
c. Calais ....
d. San Francisco ....

3

The Empire Strikes Back

15 Read what Trevor and Lena say about themselves and multi-cultural Britain.

> Hello! My name is Trevor MacDonald. I was born in Trinidad in the West Indies. I came to Britain in the 1960s. Now I am a news reader on TV.

> The first West Indians came to work in Britain in the 1950s. Today they work in nearly all sections of British life – from politics and the police to sport and music. They live in big cities like London. Every August they organise a three-day street carnival in Notting Hill, London.

> Hi! I'm Lena Aziz. My father is from Bangladesh and my mother is English. I am a presenter on a TV breakfast show.

> In the 1960s and 70s many immigrants arrived in Britain from India, Pakistan, Bangladesh and Sri Lanka. They live in cities like London, Birmingham and Bradford. A lot of Asians have their own shops and restaurants.

16 Write a sentence about each of the following, like the example.

a. Trinidad — *Trevor MacDonald was born in Trinidad.*
b. the 1950s ....
c. Notting Hill ....
d. the 1960s/70s ....
e. Bradford ....
f. shops/restaurants ....

17 Answer the questions about immigrants in your country.

a. What is (are) their country (ies) of origin?
   ....
b. When did they begin to arrive?
   ....
c. Where do they live?
   ....
d. What work do they do?
   ....

England's Greatest Writer

18 What do you know about England's greatest writer? Read the clues and complete the puzzle with the words provided.

Hamlet   poet
Richard   English
Elizabeth   Stratford
Armada   kings
actor   Earl   Saint

William **SHAKESPEARE** (1564-1616)

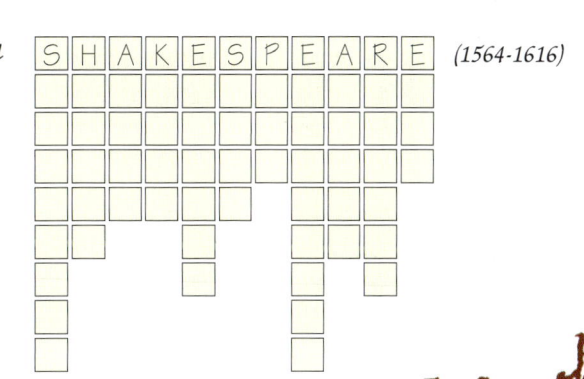

CLUES

- **s.** He was born in this town.
- **h.** One of his famous characters.
- **a.** This was his profession before he became a writer.
- **k.** He wrote many plays about these royal people.
- **e.** His work was very important for this language.
- **s.** He was born and he died on .... George's Day (April 23rd).
- **p.** He was a dramatist and a .... too.
- **e.** He was born during the reign of this queen.
- **a.** He got married in 1582 six years before the Spanish ....
- **r.** .... III is the title of one of his historical plays.
- **e.** His patron was the .... of Southampton.

19 Using the relevant information in exercise 18, write your own Pen and Ink Link about Shakespeare.

Pen and Ink Link

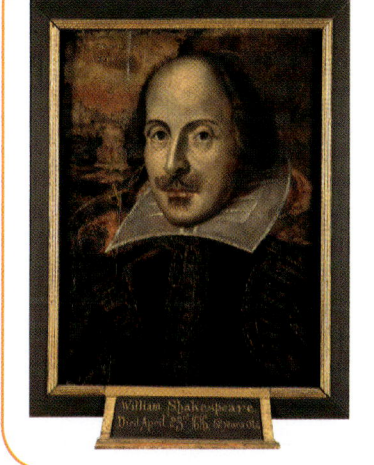

....
....
....
....
....
....
....
....

3

20 The titles for the plays below are mixed up. Write the correct title under each picture as in the example.

Romeo Caesar   **Hamlet III**
Richard and Juliet   **Julius Macbeth**

a. ☐ .... b. ☒ Richard III.............. c. ☐ ....

d. ☐ .... e. ☐ ....

21 Match the quotation from Shakespeare's play with the pictures. Write 1, 2, 3 etc. in the boxes.

1. O Romeo, Romeo wherefore art thou[1] Romeo?
2. A horse! A horse! My kingdom for a horse!
3. To be, or not to be – that is the question.
4. Friends, Romans, countrymen, lend me your ears. I come to bury Caesar, not to praise him.
5. Out, out brief candle! Life's but[2] a walking shadow…

1   **wherefore art thou**: why are you.
2   **but** : (here) only.

The Word Wizard

22 The Wizard's magic has produced word stars with countries and nationalities. Complete the sentences with the words.

> India   China
> Spain   South Africa
> Holland   Greece
> France   Ireland

> French   Dutch
> Greek   Chinese
> South African   Irish
> Spanish   Indian

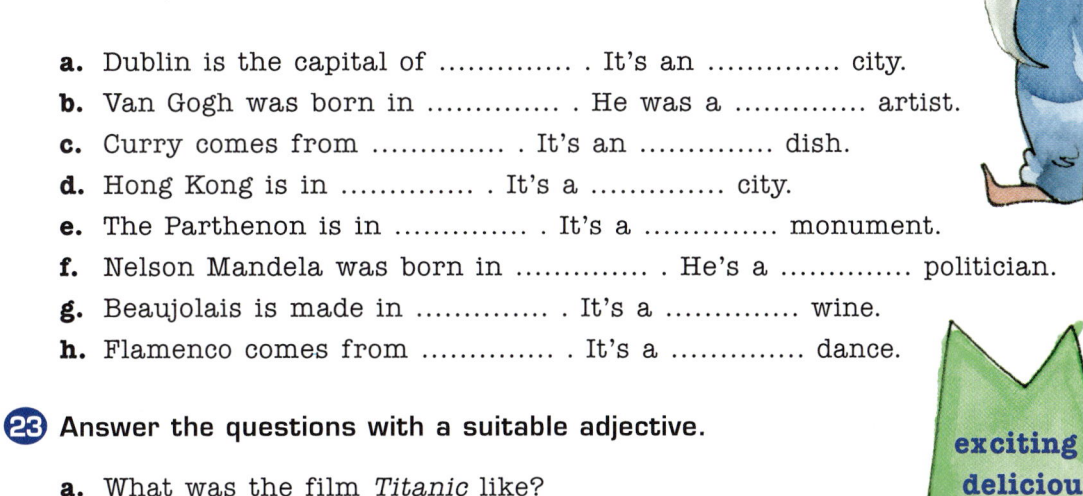

a. Dublin is the capital of .... It's an .... city.
b. Van Gogh was born in .... He was a .... artist.
c. Curry comes from .... It's an .... dish.
d. Hong Kong is in .... It's a .... city.
e. The Parthenon is in .... It's a .... monument.
f. Nelson Mandela was born in .... He's a .... politician.
g. Beaujolais is made in .... It's a .... wine.
h. Flamenco comes from .... It's a .... dance.

23 Answer the questions with a suitable adjective.

a. What was the film *Titanic* like?
....
b. You're reading *Dracula*, aren't you? What's it like?
....
c. What is Indian food like?
....
d. What is the story about the princess of death like?
....

> exciting
> delicious
> beautiful
> frightening
> unbelievable
> interesting
> horrible
> funny

24 Now write your own questions and answers using these words and a suitable adjective.

a. your holiday — What was .... ?
b. French/Italian/Chinese food — .... ?
c. English football fans — .... ?

47

3 The Grammar Ghoul

25 The Ghoul has got some 'time' words in the hour glass. Write them next to the correct preposition on the tombstone.

Words in hour glass:
1588, midnight, the 18th century, the morning, Tuesday, October, 3 o'clock, 20th November, 10th April 1962

on ....
....
in ....
....
at ....
....

26 Now complete the sentences with the correct preposition.

a. A great fire destroyed a lot of London .... 1666. It started .... Sunday September 2nd .... 2 o'clock .... the morning.

b. Every year .... November 5th the British celebrate Guy Fawkes' Night in the streets or their gardens .... night. .... 1605 Guy Fawkes tried to blow up the Houses of Parliament and kill the king, but he was arrested.

c. The Grammar Ghoul was born .... midnight .... December 31st, 1890.

27 When were YOU born? Write the time (if you know!), day, month and year.

I was born ....

28 The Ghoul's knife is dripping blood over the adjectives in these sentences. Write the superlative form of the words provided below in the correct sentence.

famous   strange   big   great   safe   ~~horrible~~

a. The Grammar Ghoul is the most *horrible* ghoul in the world.

b. People say that Shakespeare is the .... writer in English.

c. In the 19th century Britain had the .... empire in the world.

d. 'The Princess of Death' is one of the .... stories about the *Titanic*.

e. Trevor MacDonald is the most .... news reader in Britain.

f. People believed that the *Titanic* was the .... ship in the world.

➡ Now turn to page 93 for the Revision Test.

48

Mystery Stop 4

What is the name of the city?
Read the clues and look at the map on page 6.

> From Southampton go north-east towards the River Thames.
> The city has got two 'o's and two 'n's in it.

The city is called ……………………………… .

Lord Lyttleton.

1 What was the mysterious terror in a London house? Read and listen to the page from Lord Lyttleton's book *Notes and Queries* (1879).

Very strange things have happened at 50 Berkeley Square. Some years ago a terrified maid* lost her mind. She is now in a hospital for lunatics. One morning another maid was found on the floor, talking to herself in terror. She died in hospital later that day. Then a girl who was a guest in the house went mad. And a man died in the night in the bedroom on the second floor.

Berkeley Square in the 1860s.

Sir Robert Warboys stayed in the house one night. He didn't believe in ghosts but he took a gun with him. After he went to bed there was a shot. His friends found him dead in the second-floor bedroom. There was an expression of terror on his face.

I have spent a night in the same room. I had two guns with me. During the night I fired one of them at a dark ghostly shape* which was coming towards me. It vanished and I survived*. But I was very disturbed. Since that night I have had bad dreams.

2 Now match the two parts of the sentences. Write a, b, c etc. in the boxes.

a. One maid
b. Another maid
c. A girl guest
d. A man
e. Sir Robert Warboys
f. Lord Lyttleton

1. ☐ died during the night.
2. ☐ survived but was very disturbed.
3. ☐ is in a hospital for lunatics.
4. ☐ went mad.
5. ☐ died of terror.
6. ☐ died in hospital.

4

3 Underline the correct form of the verb.

a. Very strange things (*have happened/happened*) at 50 Berkeley Square.
b. Some years ago a maid (*has lost/lost*) her mind.
c. One night Sir Robert Warboys (*died/has died*) in the second-floor bedroom.
d. Lord Lyttleton (*spent/has spent*) a night in the same room.
e. During the night he (*has seen/saw*) something.
f. Since then he (*has had/had*) bad dreams.

4 Listen to Robert Martin's statement about his frightening experience in the same house. Then complete the statement with the words in the box. Listen again and check your answers.

so   and   when   but   because   then   and   when

METROPOLITAN POLICE STATEMENT

Date: December 25th 1887
Time: 5:20 am

Name: Robert Martin
Age: 27
Occupation: sailor

Edward Blunden and I are sailors from Portsmouth. ¹........................ we arrived in London last night we walked around the streets ².......................... we couldn't find a place to sleep. We saw a TO LET* notice outside 50 Berkeley Square ³......................... went in. The house was empty ⁴.......................... we decided to sleep in a room on the second floor.
I fell asleep quickly ⁵......................... Blunden woke me up. He said he could hear footsteps coming slowly towards the door.
⁶......................... a dark shape entered the room. Blunden was trying to get something heavy from the fireplace ⁷......................... the thing attacked him. I ran out in panic. I saw a policeman in the street ⁸......................... we went back to the house. Blunden was dead. His neck was broken. His eyes were open wide with terror.

This statement is true.

Signed

Robert Martin

50

5 Listen to the letter from Peggy Hodgson to the 'Society for Psychic Research' about poltergeist activity in her house in London. Number the items in the order they are mentioned. Write 1, 2, 3 etc. in the boxes.

a. □ b. □ c. □ d. □ e. □

6 Now read the letter and underline the verbs that are in the Present Perfect tense and circle the verbs in the Past Simple.

Enfield
North London

10th September 1979

Dear Sirs,

Since we came to live in this house some very strange things have happened. For example, many times my 11-year-old daughter Janet has heard footsteps walking in slippers across her bedroom and loud knocks on the wall. And even a heavy bed has moved twice. I've seen a hairbrush flying in the air. It hit my son Billy on the head. When a policewoman came she saw a chair flying across the room.

Janet has woken up screaming several times. She said something threw her in the air. One night her sister Margaret was nearly strangled by a curtain.

We have had these strange happenings for two years and they haven't stopped yet. What can we do?

Yours faithfully,

Peggy Hodgson (Mrs)

7 Use the verbs from question 6 to make questions for the answers on the right.

a. What .... ? Footsteps and loud knocks.
b. How many times .... ? Twice.
c. What .... ? A chair flying across the room.
d. Who .... ? Margaret.
e. How long .... ? For two years.
f. When .... ? In 1977.

4

Mystery History

8 Read the brochure and write the names of the places on the river.

9 Are these sentences true (T) or false (F)? Correct the false ones.

                                                                                              T   F

a. The river trip starts at Tower Bridge and ends at Hampton Court.

b. The Magna Carta gave freedom to more people.

c. William the Conqueror built the Tower to protect his people.

d. The first 'parliament' met in the House of Commons.

e. Since 1660 Parliament has had real authority.

f. Many English monarchs have been buried* in Westminster Abbey.

4

Take a riverboat trip to Runnymede and discover how England became the Mother of Parliaments

Departure: Tower Bridge Pier, 9.30am.
Return: Tower Bridge Pier, 6.00pm.

Join us on a river trip to Runnymede, near Windsor. The first stop is the Tower of London, begun by William the Conqueror in 1078. The fortress was a symbol of royal power over a conquered land.

The next stop is Westminster Hall, situated in the Houses of Parliament, where the first 'parliament' was assembled* by the baron Simon de Montfort in 1265.

Your tour continues with a visit to the Houses of Parliament, the mother of parliamentary democracy. When Charles II became king in 1660, he was a 'constitutional' monarch. Since then the real authority in England has always been Parliament.

Next you will visit Westminster Abbey, behind the Houses of Parliament, completed in 1065. Since 1066 the Abbey has seen every royal coronation. Many kings and queens are buried* there.

The trip includes a stop at Hampton Court, Henry VIII's splendid palace with its world-famous maze*. Lunch will be served on the boat.

Last stop Runnymede, just before Windsor. Here in 1215 the barons forced King John to sign the Great Charter (Magna Carta). This gave more people liberties and privileges.

4

🎧 15 ⓵⓪ Listen to the recording about some ghosts that haunt the Tower of London and complete the table. The first one is done for you.

Year	Who?	Age	Ghost seen
1483	Edward V	12 ½	✓
......	...... Duke of York	......	......
......	Sir Thomas More	?	......
......	...... Boleyn	......	......
......	Catherine Howard	......	......
......	...... Grey	......	......

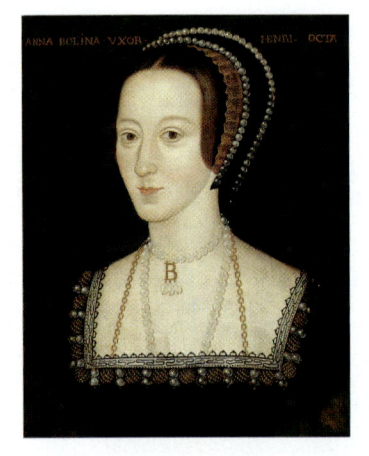

Anne Boleyn by unknown artist.
By courtesy of the
National Portrait Gallery, London.

Called Catherine Howard
by unknown artist.
By courtesy of the
National Portrait Gallery, London.

Called Lady Jane Dudley
(née Grey) by unknown artist.
By courtesy of the
National Portrait Gallery, London.

⓵⓵ Now answer the questions. (Listen again if necessary.)

　a. Who ordered the murder of the two princes?
　b. Where have their ghosts appeared?
　c. Why was Sir Thomas More executed?
　d. Who walks the Tower walls at night?
　e. When did guards see the ghost of Lady Jane Grey?

⓵② Write a short guide saying where the Tower ghosts have been seen.

　Begin like this: *The Bloody Tower is haunted by several ghosts ...*

TIMECHART

13 Use the timechart to underline the correct answer in the summary.

The Age of Expansion

AD
1688-9	The Glorious Revolution. Dutch Protestant William III and his wife Mary are invited to succeed deposed Catholic James II. Bill of Rights establishes Protestant liberties.
1714	George I is called from Hanover, Germany.
1715	First Jacobite rebellion by James Edward Stuart (son of James II) defeated.
1721	Robert Walpole becomes England's first Prime Minister.
1746	Second Jacobite rebellion led by Charles Edward Stuart (grandson of James II) defeated at Culloden.
1756-63	The Seven Years War with France. Ends with Britain's victory and more colonies in India and America.
1776	Declaration of America's independence.
1783	Britain recognises American independence. William Pitt becomes Prime Minister at the age of 24.

The Glorious Revolution established Britain as a (*Catholic/Protestant*) country. The Jacobite rebels of 1715 and 1746 wanted a (*Catholic/Protestant*) monarchy but they were defeated. The Hanoverians, like (*William III/George I*), were German Protestants. In 1763 the British Empire was expanding, but (*10/20*) years later the (*American/West Indian*) colonies were lost. Parliament and English democracy became much stronger and produced some very good (*soldiers/Prime Ministers*) like Walpole and Pitt.

William III, Prince of Orange arriving at Brixham by unknown artist.
The Royal Collection © 2000, Her Majesty Queen Elizabeth II.

The Parliament Fun Quiz

14 What do you know about the British Parliament? Circle the correct answer.

1. Members of Parliament (MPs) are elected in a general election
   a. annually
   b. by the Royal Family
   c. every 5 years

2. The two main political parties in Britain are
   a. the Liberal Democrats/ the Greens
   b. the Labour Party/ the Conservative Party
   c. the Communist Party/ the Nationalist Party

3. The leader of the winning party is called
   a. Big Ben
   b. the Prime Minister
   c. the President

4. He or she usually lives at
   a. 10 Downing Street
   b. Buckingham Palace
   c. the Houses of Parliament

5. The losing political party is called
   a. the Opposition
   b. the Government
   c. the Cabinet

6. Who is the formal head of both Houses of Parliament?
   a. the Duke of Edinburgh
   b. the Prince of Wales
   c. the Queen

15 Use the information in the text to complete the chart about three of London's bridges.

London Bridge is depicted in the background *c.* 1415.

The Romans first built a wooden bridge over the Thames in the second half of the 1st century AD. In 1014 Saxons and Vikings burnt down London Bridge in a battle. The first stone bridge was constructed in 1176, and by 1200 there were houses on it. This bridge remained for over 600 years. The heads of executed people – for example, Sir Thomas More – were put on the gatehouse. In 1598 a German tourist counted thirty heads on the bridge.

For centuries London had only one bridge, so people also crossed the river by boat. Then in 1750 a second bridge was opened, called Westminster Bridge. A new London Bridge was completed in 1831. This was demolished in 1967 and rebuilt in the USA. The modern bridge was opened in 1973.

Tower Bridge was built down river from London Bridge in 1894. The road over the bridge is built on bascules, movable sections of road which open two or three times a week to let ships pass.

Tower Bridge.

AD	
43-100	....
1014	....
1176-1200	....
1598	....
1750	....
1831	....
1894	....
1967	....
1973	....

4

Time Out in London

16 Read the information below and match the five sentences on page 59 with the advertisements. Write a, b, c etc. in the boxes.

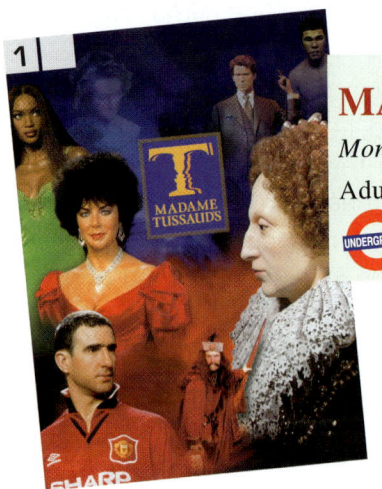

MADAME TUSSAUD'S
Mon-Fri 10am - 5.30 pm
Adult £9.00 / Child (5-15) £6.00
UNDERGROUND Baker Street

the London Dungeon
Open Mon-Sun 10am - 5.30pm
Adult £9.00 / Child (up to 14) £6.50
UNDERGROUND London Bridge

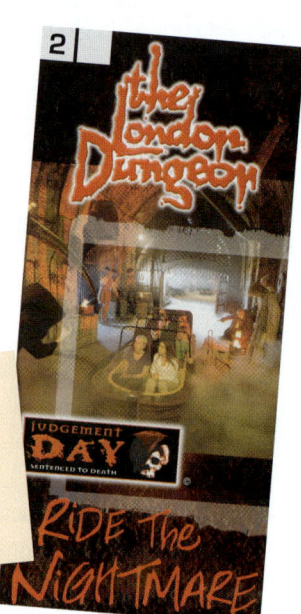

ROCK CIRCUS
Mon-Fri 11am - 9pm
Adult £8.50 / Child (5-16) £7.00
UNDERGROUND Piccadilly Circus

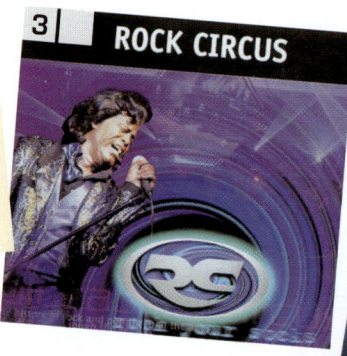

MAMMA MIA!
Prince Edward, Old Compton Street
Mon-Sat 7.30pm
Prices £15 - £35.00
UNDERGROUND Leicester Square

London Aquarium
Open Mon-Fri 10am - 6pm
Adult £7.00 / Child (3-14) £5.00
UNDERGROUND Westminster

Match the sentences with the correct advertisements.

a. Experience a nightmare* tour of the dark side of London.
b. Touch the ray fish* and join the sharks for lunch!
c. A new musical based on the songs of ABBA.
d. Come and say hello to the Good, the Bad, the Beautiful and the Ugly.
e. Visit the world's number one rock attraction and experience fifty years of British rock history.

17 Now answer the questions.

a. What is the nearest underground station for the London Aquarium?
b. Which attraction closes at 9 o'clock in the evening?
c. If you are under 14, how much do you pay for The London Dungeon?
d. What time does *Mamma Mia!* start?
e. Where can you see a lot of famous people?

18 Complete the mini-dialogues with the verbs in the boxes. Use the Past Simple or Present Perfect forms.

a. You: .... the show .... yet?
Usher: No, it starts in five minutes. Have you got a ticket?
You: No, can I buy one now?
Usher: Sorry, somebody .... the last ticket a few moments ago.

> **start   buy**

b. You: Where .... you .... ?
Friend: The London Aquarium.
You: .... you .... it?
Friend: Yes, it .... great!

> **like   be (x2)**

c. Friend: I've got two tickets for Madame Tussaud's. Would you like to come?
You: Sorry, I .... already .... there.
Friend: What .... it like?
You: Fantastic! But I .... to the Chamber of Horrors. I was too scared*!

> **be (x2)   (not) go**

19 Now write your own dialogue for one of the advertisements on page 58.

20 These sentences are NOT grammatically correct. Can you write the corrections?

a. The Hodgson family lived in their house since 1977.
b. I have seen Ann Boleyn's ghost last night.
c. The strange happenings have begun two years ago.
d. Did you visit Westminster Abbey yet?
e. There has been a ghost here a moment ago but now it went.
(**Two mistakes!**)

Pen and Ink Link

21 Use the information on the book covers to complete the text.

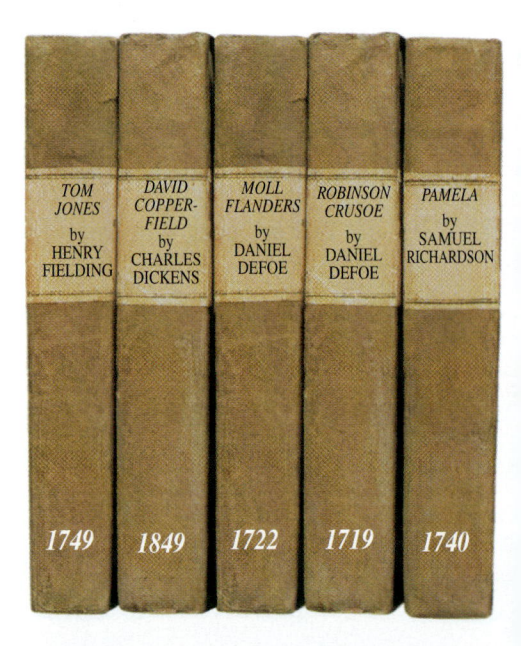

Journalist Daniel Defoe (1660-1731) was a pioneer of the English novel. After his most famous book, [1].................... (1719), he wrote [2].................... (1722), about the life of a woman who becomes a thief.

Samuel Richardson's novel [3].................... ([4]......) contains the letters of a teenage servant girl defending her virtue against her employer's son.

A different novel is [5]..........................'s *Tom Jones* ([6]......). His hero is not virtuous like Pamela, but he is kind and honest.

Born in Portsmouth, England's greatest novelist Charles Dickens (1812-70) spent most of his early life in London, so he knew the city very well. Many of his novels, like *Oliver Twist* (1839) are set in London. He wrote 13 great novels, including [7]..................... ([8]......).

Daniel Defoe
by Michiel Van der Gucht
(1660-1725).
By courtesy of the
National Portrait Gallery, London.

Charles Dickens (1839)
by Daniel Maclise (1806-1870).
By courtesy of the National Portrait Gallery, London.

The Word Wizard

22 The Wizard has made two puffs of smoke with occupations and places of work. Can you match them, like the example?

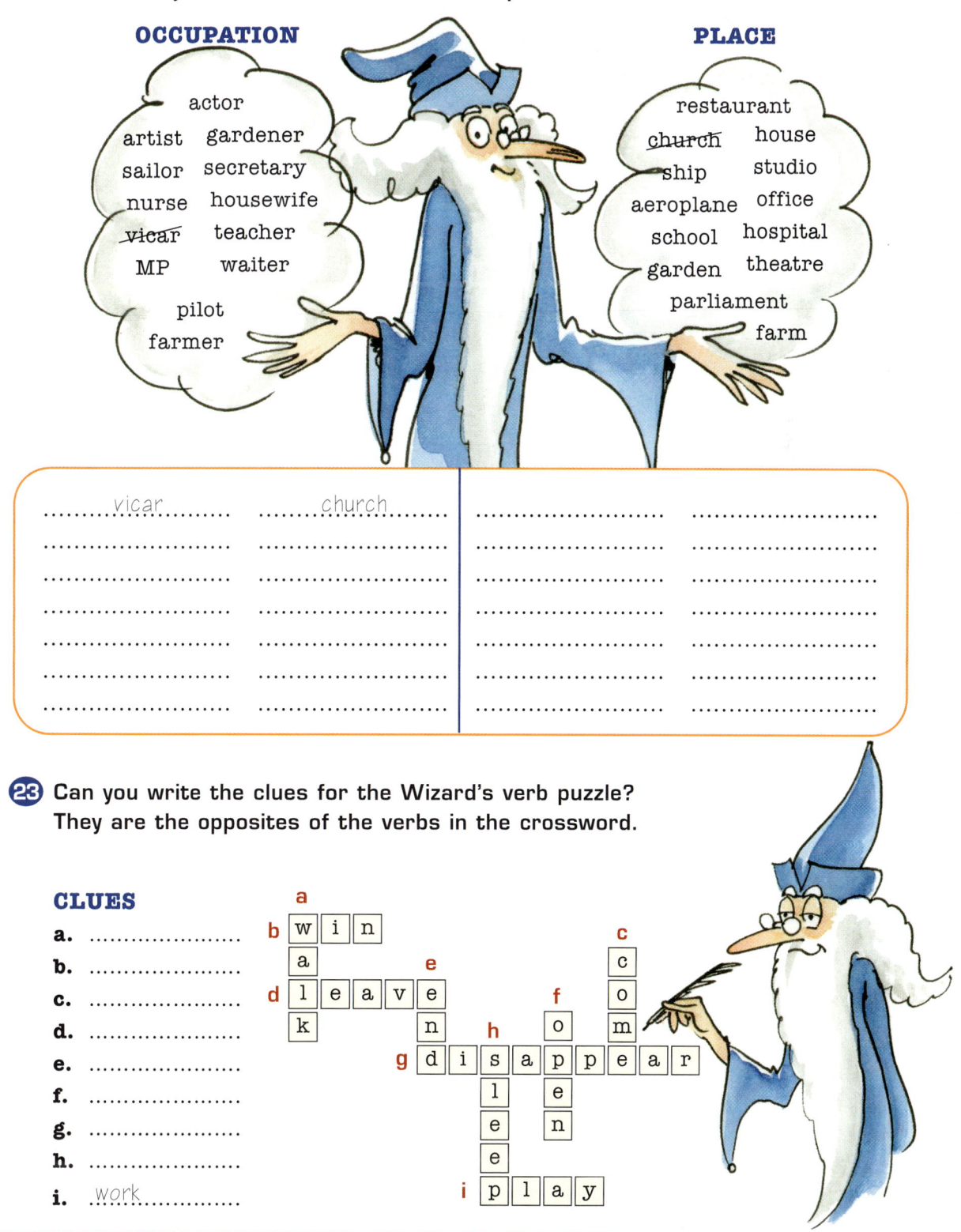

OCCUPATION: actor, artist, gardener, sailor, secretary, nurse, housewife, vicar, teacher, MP, waiter, pilot, farmer

PLACE: restaurant, church, house, ship, studio, aeroplane, office, school, hospital, garden, theatre, parliament, farm

......vicar......	......church......	....	....
....	....	....	....
....	....	....	....
....	....	....	....
....	....	....	....
....	....	....	....
....	....	....	....

23 Can you write the clues for the Wizard's verb puzzle? They are the opposites of the verbs in the crossword.

CLUES
a. ....
b. ....
c. ....
d. ....
e. ....
f. ....
g. ....
h. ....
i. ......work......

Crossword answers:
- b. win
- d. leave
- g. disappear
- i. play
- a. (down) ask
- e. (down) even
- c. (down) come
- f. (down) open
- h. (down) please (asleep)

4 The Grammar Ghoul

24 The Ghoul is having a party with some friends. What are they saying? Complete the bubbles with the verbs in the box. Use the imperative form – positive (✓) and negative (-).

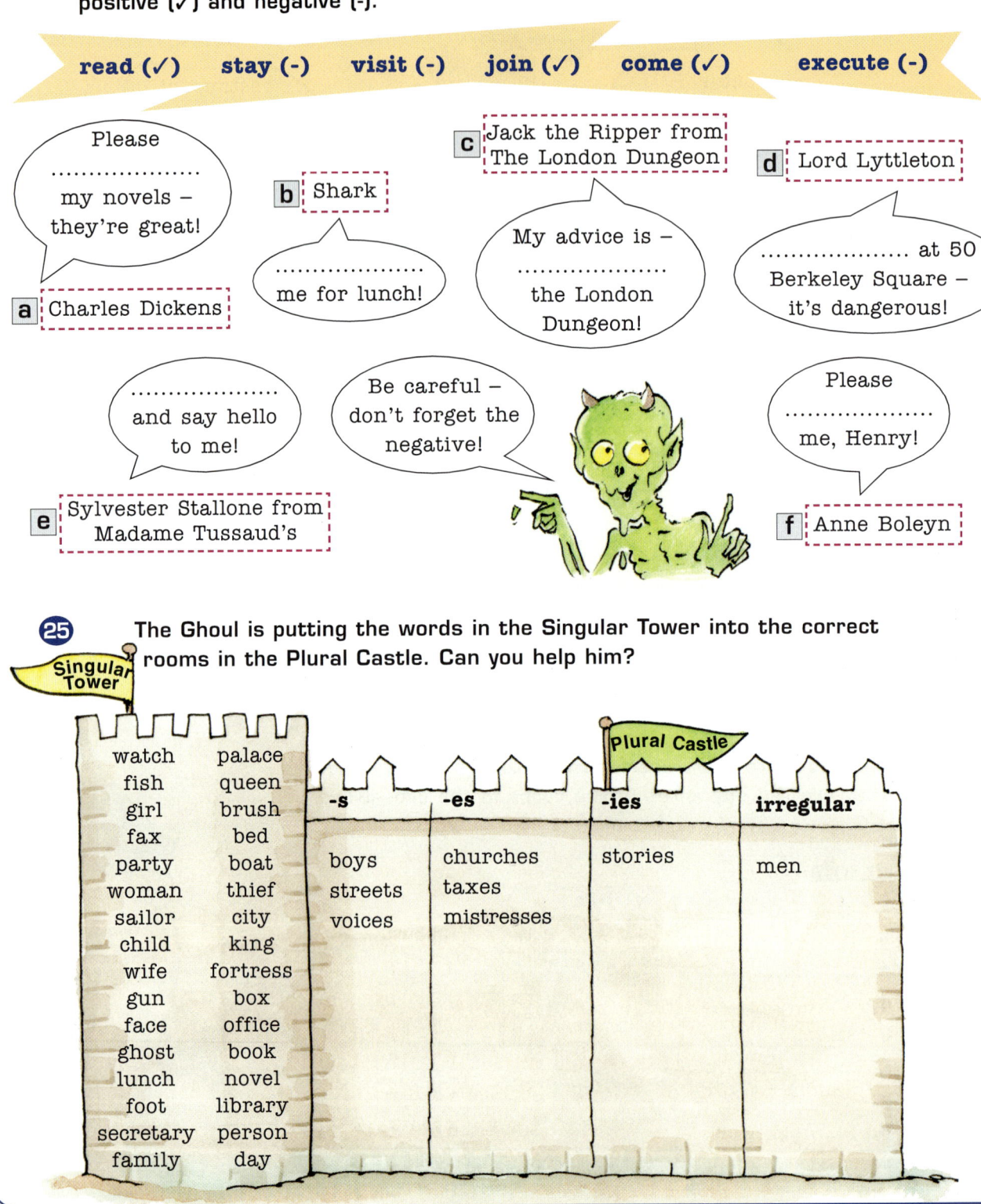

read (✓)   stay (-)   visit (-)   join (✓)   come (✓)   execute (-)

a **Charles Dickens**: Please .... my novels – they're great!

b **Shark**: .... me for lunch!

c **Jack the Ripper from The London Dungeon**: My advice is – .... the London Dungeon!

d **Lord Lyttleton**: .... at 50 Berkeley Square – it's dangerous!

e **Sylvester Stallone from Madame Tussaud's**: .... and say hello to me!

(Ghoul): Be careful – don't forget the negative!

f **Anne Boleyn**: Please .... me, Henry!

25 The Ghoul is putting the words in the Singular Tower into the correct rooms in the Plural Castle. Can you help him?

Singular Tower: watch, fish, girl, fax, party, woman, sailor, child, wife, gun, face, ghost, lunch, foot, secretary, family, palace, queen, brush, bed, boat, thief, city, king, fortress, box, office, book, novel, library, person, day

Plural Castle:

-s	-es	-ies	irregular
boys	churches	stories	men
streets	taxes		
voices	mistresses		

➡ Now turn to page 94 for the Revision Test.

62

Mystery Stop 5

What is the name of the city? Read the clues and look at the map on page 6.

> Go north from London.
> The city has a famous university.

Complete the name of the city. Cam.................

1 Listen to Matthew Manning talking about his psychic experiences to the pupils of a school in Cambridge and put the pictures in chronological order using the dates below (1-6).

a ☐   b ☐   c ☐

d ☐   e ☐   f ☐

1. 1955
3. Summer 1971
5. 1974
2. 1967
4. November 1971
6. 1980

2 What *can* or *can't* Matthew do with his psychic powers? Write the words in the correct part of the table. Listen again to the text in exercise 1, if necessary.

> heal* sick people
> travel to other planets   see ghosts   write pop songs
> make himself invisible   speak to aliens   bend* metal
> perform magic tricks   draw pictures automatically
> make objects fly   win card games   predict the future
> write messages in many languages   win the lottery
> make objects appear and disappear   move furniture

Can
Can't

3 Using the table, write three sentences with *can/can't*, like this example.

He can see ghosts but he can't speak to aliens.

4 Read and listen to the strange case of the Scottish nanny.

The nanny in the 'Spooky-fires' case arrives home a free woman – but is she a witch?

Scottish nanny Carol Compton arrived home last night after 16 months in prison. 21-year-old Carol was put on trial* in Livorno, Italy, this month for arson (causing fires) and attempted murder*. The Italian media and public were very interested in the case because some people believe Carol is a witch!

In August 1982 Carol was arrested on the island of Elba where she worked as a nanny for a family. There were two fires in the family home; one nearly killed a 3-year-old child called Agnese. A forensic expert from Pisa said they weren't normal fires. They burned downwards not up, and they were caused by heat not flames. Other strange things happened when Carol was around. A vase and a picture of the Madonna fell on the floor. Agnese's grandmother said a plate and a cake dish fell off the table. But the prosecution* did not want to include accusations of witchcraft* or the paranormal in the case. Carol was found guilty of arson and sentenced to 2 1/2 years in prison. But she was released immediately because she had already been in prison for 16 months.

Carol Compton in Livorno.

5 Are these statements true (T) or false (F)? Correct the false ones.

	T	F
a. Carol was put on trial 16 months after her arrest.	☐	☐
b. The media thought she was a witch.	☐	☐
c. She worked for an Italian family in Livorno.	☐	☐
d. The family thought she had tried to kill Agnese by fire.	☐	☐
e. The forensic expert thought the fires were unusual.	☐	☐
f. Carol seemed to have paranormal powers.	☐	☐
g. The prosecution accused Carol of witchcraft.	☐	☐
h. Carol spent 2 1/2 years in prison.	☐	☐

Was Carol a witch? What is your conclusion?

6 Find words in the text which match these definitions.

a. Radio, TV, newspapers etc. ....
b. A person (usually a woman) with supernatural powers. ....
c. The crime of causing fires. ....
d. Describes somebody or something from Scotland. ....
e. A place where criminals are locked away. ....
f. A legal process which examines the cause of a crime. ....

7 Can you write the definitions for these words?

a. Italian ....
b. murder ....
c. nanny ....
d. guilty ....

The strange case of the Scottish nanny

5

Mystery History

8 Read the dialogue between you and a ghost and then answer the questions below.

You: Who are you?

Ghost: My name is Matthew Hopkins. During my life I was a famous witch-hunter. They called me the witchfinder general.

You: What do you want?

Ghost: I want to confess the terrible things I did from 1645 to 1647. I interrogated and tortured hundreds of witches. Many of them were executed.

You: Where?

Ghost: It began in my village – Manningtree in Essex. Nineteen witches were hanged. Then the witch-hunt moved to Suffolk and Cambridgeshire. There were nearly 200 trials. Many witches died.

You: How did you know they were witches?

Ghost: I found the witch's mark on them.

You: What's that?

Ghost: It's the place on the witch's body where her 'familiars' suck her blood. 'Familiars' are demons in the form of an animal – a mouse, dog, cat, rabbit…

You: But what wrong did these women do?

Ghost: They made a pact with the devil. He offered them money or revenge* on their enemies. In return they gave him their body and soul.

You: Did you get any money for your work?

Ghost: Yes. About £6 per witch.

You: So you made a lot of money. Why did the witch-hunt stop in 1647?

Ghost: I died of tuberculosis. And now, after 360 years, I can rest in peace!

a. What did Hopkins do between 1645 and 1647?
b. What happened to the witches?
c. Where did the witch-hunt happen?
d. How many witches were tried?
e. How did Hopkins know they were witches?
f. What are a witch's 'familiars'?
g. Who offered the witches money or revenge?
h. Why did the witch-hunt stop in 1647?

Matthew Hopkins the witch-hunter.

9 Using the information in the leaflet, complete the route in red and number the places (2-9).

Mystery Walk Number 3. Time 1½ Hours.

1. Peterhouse. The oldest College in Cambridge. Founded in 1284.

2. The Eagle pub, Bene't Street. Here, scientists Francis Crick and James Watson discussed their ideas about DNA, the genetic code. They received the Nobel Prize in 1962.

3. King's College Chapel. This beautiful building was founded by Henry VI and begun in 1446.

4. The Backs. Lawns* and gardens belonging to the colleges. Open to the public.

5. Clare Bridge. The oldest surviving bridge in Cambridge. Built 1638-40.

6. Senate House. 18th-century building where Degree* Day (an annual ceremony when students receive their degrees) takes place.

7. Trinity College has Sir Christopher Wren's library with works by Milton and a first folio of Shakespeare.

8. Bridge of Sighs. Built in 1831 in the style of the famous bridge in Venice.

9. Magdalene Bridge. The first bridge over the River Cam was built on this site before 875 AD.

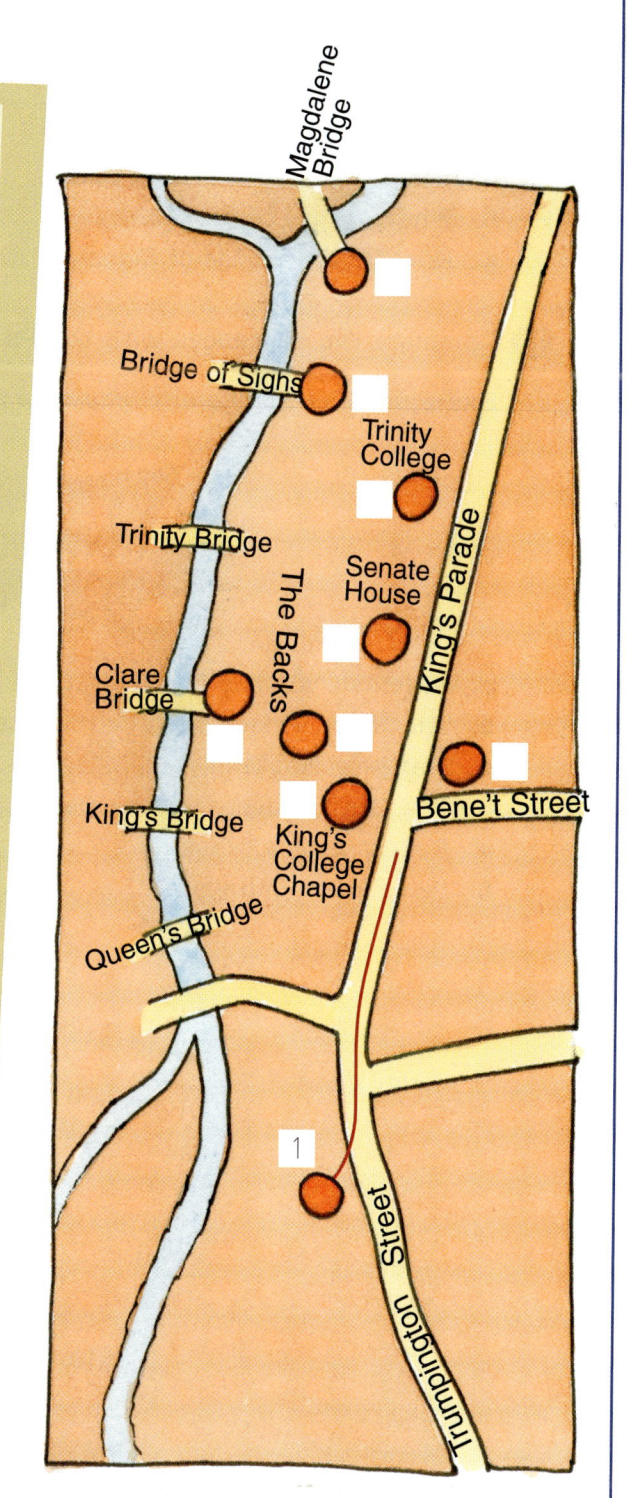

10 Complete the spaces with a question or an answer.

a. Where does the mystery walk begin? ....
b. Who .... ? Crick and Watson.
c. When was King's College Chapel begun? ....
d. What .... ? Lawns and gardens belonging to the colleges.
e. When was Clare Bridge built? ....
f. Where .... ? The Senate House.
g. How did the Bridge of Sighs get its name? ....

11 Complete the sentences with the Past Simple Passive form of the verbs.

Example: *The Bridge of Sighs **was built** in 1831.*

award*   pay   try
hang   build   found

a. Nineteen witches .... in Manningtree, Essex. (*Careful!*)
b. The Nobel Prize .... to Crick and Watson.
c. Matthew Hopkins .... £6 for each witch.
d. The first bridge over the Cam .... before 875 AD.
e. Nearly 200 witches .... between 1645-7. (*Careful!*)
f. Peterhouse College .... in 1284.

OXFORD VS. CAMBRIDGE

The first boat race between Oxford and Cambridge was in 1829 on the Thames. Since 1856 they have raced every year from Putney Bridge to Mortlake (4 1/2 miles). By 1982 Cambridge had won 68 races, Oxford 59, and once they finished at exactly the same time. In 1912 both boats sank!

12 Behind the masks are four famous students from Cambridge University. Complete the bubbles with the correct name.

> **Charles Darwin (1809-82)**   **Sir Isaac Newton (1642-1727)**
> **Charles, Prince of Wales (1948-)**   **Oliver Cromwell (1599-1658)**

a. I began studying at Trinity College in 1967 and I graduated in 1970 with a degree in history. I am the first heir* to the throne to get a degree*. Who am I?
....

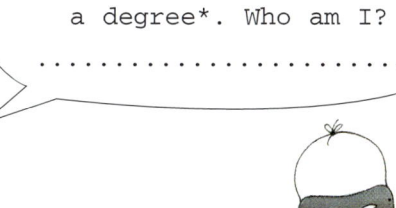

b. I studied mathematics at Trinity College and became Professor of Mathematics there in 1668 when I was 26. I discovered the laws of gravity after an apple fell on my head! Who am I?
....

c. I was at Christ's College from 1828-31, and then I travelled round the world as a naturalist on *The Beagle*. In 1859 I published *The Origin of Species*, a book about evolution. Who am I?
....

d. I was 17 when I went to Sussex College in 1616. I became an MP and helped to execute Charles I. I was Lord Protector of England. In 1960 my head was buried in the chapel of my college. Who am I?
....

13 What about Oxford University? Do you know these famous people?

a. Lewis Carroll, author of Alice in Wonderland.
b. Percy Bysshe Shelley, poet.
c. ....
d. Lawrence of Arabia,
e. ....

5

And finally...

BRITAIN'S YOUNGEST CHILD PRODIGY

In 1981 Ruth Lawrence won a mathematics scholarship* to Oxford. She was 10 years old. In 1983 Ruth got a first class degree in mathematics and immediately began studying for a doctorate. Her father Harry, a computer consultant, instructed her from an early age and helped her to become Britain's most brilliant maths student.

14 Now answer these questions.

a. Why is Newton famous?
   ....

b. Which university did Prince Charles go to?
   ....

c. How old was Ruth Lawrence when she got her degree?
   ....

d. Which female Prime Minister went to Oxford?
   ....

e. What is Darwin's theory called?
   ....

15 Think of a famous person (from abroad or your own country, dead or alive) and write down what you know about him/her. Then ask your partner to guess who the person is.

TIMECHART

16 Read the text and complete your own timechart.

The Age of Industrialism

AD
1793 ....
1815 ....
1825 ....
1829 ....
1831 ....
1837 ....
1840 ....
1851 ....

During this period Britain was at war with France for about 20 years. The war began in 1793 and ended when Napoleon was finally defeated in 1815 at the Battle of Waterloo. The first railway opened in 1825, and the first police force was established in 1829. The first cheap postage stamp (the Penny Black) was used in 1840. Michael Faraday discovered electricity in 1831. Queen Victoria's long reign began in 1837. And in 1851 Britain's industrial and economic progress was displayed* at the Great Exhibition in Hyde Park.

Pen and Ink Link

17 Listen and fill in the gaps.

The Cambridge Romantics

Name: Lord Byron
Year of birth: [1]...... .
Education: Trinity College ([2]......-......)
Life: Travelled in Spain and [3].................. .
Lived in [4].................. .
Died: [5]......, helping Greek struggle* against Turks.
Masterpiece/Most famous work:
[6].................. (1819-24 Unfinished).

Name: William Wordsworth
Year of birth: [1]...... .
Education: St John's College ([2]......-......)
Life: Inspired by French Revolution. Wrote *Lyrical Ballads* with Coleridge and founded English Romanticism. Lived in the [3].................. . Poet Laureate ([4]......).
Died: [5]...... .
Masterpiece/Most famous work: *The Prelude*.

Name: Samuel Taylor Coleridge
Year of birth: [1]...... .
Education: Jesus College ([2]......-......)
Life: Poet, critic, philosopher. His literary partnership with Wordsworth founded English Romanticism. Became addicted to [3].................. .
Died: [4]...... .
Masterpiece/Most famous work: *The Rime of the Ancient Mariner* and *Kubla Khan* (unfinished).

5 Education in Britain

18 Follow the road of the British education system and then put the sentences in the correct order. Write 1, 2, 3 etc. in the boxes.

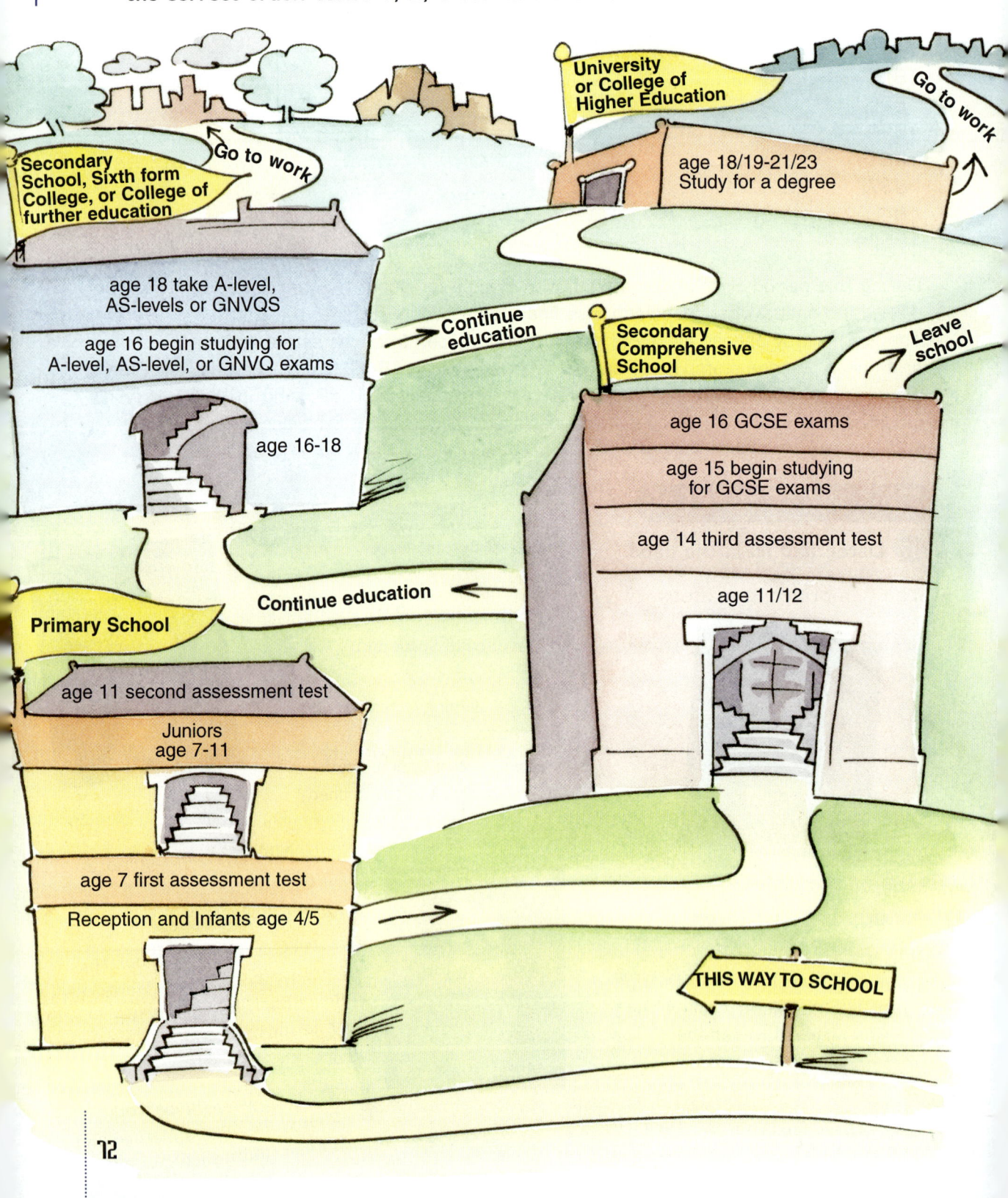

University or College of Higher Education
age 18/19-21/23 Study for a degree
Go to work

Secondary School, Sixth form College, or College of further education
Go to work
age 18 take A-level, AS-levels or GNVQS
age 16 begin studying for A-level, AS-level, or GNVQ exams
age 16-18

Continue education

Secondary Comprehensive School
Leave school
age 16 GCSE exams
age 15 begin studying for GCSE exams
age 14 third assessment test
age 11/12

Continue education

Primary School
age 11 second assessment test
Juniors age 7-11
age 7 first assessment test
Reception and Infants age 4/5

THIS WAY TO SCHOOL

72

a. ☐ When they are 7 years old they take the first assessment test*.
b. ☐ Then they can leave school or stay on.
c. ☐ After that they go on to secondary school.
d. ☐ At 15 they start studying for the General Certificate of Secondary Education exams (GCSEs).
e. ☐ Finally, they can go to work or continue their education at university or a college of higher education.
f. ☐ British children start primary school at 4 (Reception or Foundation class) or 5 (infant class) years old.
g. ☐ They take the GCSEs at 16.
h. ☐ Then they continue in the juniors.
i. ☐ They do the third assessment test at 14.
j. ☐ If pupils stay at school from 16-18, they study for Advanced (A) levels or Greater National Vocational Qualifications (GNVQs).
k. ☐ At 11 they take the second assessment test.

19 Using sentences a-k in exercise 18 as a model, briefly describe the education system in your country.

20 Listen to and read the article below. Complete the tables on the next page with information from the magazine article.

A NATION OF TRIVIA* ADDICTS?

According to a recent survey*, 83% of Britain's population read for less than 3 hours a day. So what do people read? About 4 million of us consume a diet of gossip* and trivia in the tabloids* (*The Sun, The Mirror*). That's about four times the number for quality papers (*The Times, The Guardian*), which contain important news.

Alarming? Yes – when you think that the most popular books are crime stories, thrillers, and romance – a high-cholesterol menu of sex and violence.

The truth is we are a nation of trivia addicts. Most people spend their free time in front of the TV. So do we watch programmes that exercise the brain? No hope. The top programmes are soaps. *Coronation Street* is number one with 14.84 million viewers a week. A close second is *Eastenders* with 14.71 million. And if that's not enough junk* food, you can feast on *Emmerdale Farm*, *Neighbours*, *Brookside*, etc. etc. It seems that we can't eat enough of this sticky porridge* of trivia.

Obesity of the body is a big problem. Obesity of the mind is a serious problem. It's a terminal illness.

5

What do we read?   **What do we watch?**

Tabloids	Contain	No. of readers	Top five soaps	Audience in millions
.... The Sun	popular news	4 million	1.	....
Quality papers The Times	....	....	2. .... 3. *Emmerdale* 4.	.... 12.01 10.56
Books	....		5. *Brookside*	8.25

21 Shelly is talking about some of her favourite things. Listen and write a heading for each column. Then listen again and use the suggestions below to write one sentence in each yellow column.

Top of the Pops	Shout	White Fang

great music
favourite bands
loves dogs
interesting topics
photo-stories
dog story

22 Now complete the green columns with <u>your</u> favourite things and tell the class.

The Word Wizard

23 Circle the word that is different from the others, like the example. Then choose the appropriate category from the words provided.

countries   female people   public buildings   animals
university   school subjects   parts of a house   reading material

a. mathematics   car   history   art — school subjects
b. witch   library   pub   school — ....
c. mouse   dog   cat   money — ....
d. picture   book   magazine   newspaper — ....
e. roof   window   bridge   floor — ....
f. France   Britain   river   Spain — ....
g. girl   grandmother   queen   garden — ....
h. college   trial   degree   student — ....

24 Put the words in the correct lens of the wizard's glasses. Be careful, some might go in both lenses.

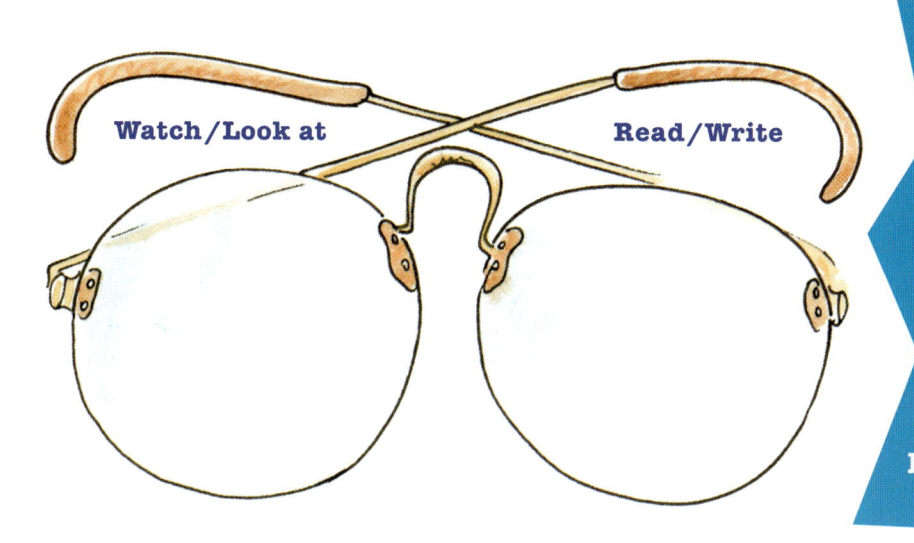

Watch/Look at   **Read/Write**

poem   message   photo   document   tabloid   boat race   film   school report   video cassette   drawing   magazine   football match   crossword puzzle   exam   painting   letter   soap opera   leaflet   magic trick   documentary

25 Now match some of the words with their definitions.

a. A written or printed paper containing facts or proof. — document
b. A paper containing questions for pupils or students. — ....
c. A picture made with a camera. — ....
d. A popular newspaper. — ....

Can you write definitions for two more words?

The Grammar Ghoul

26 The ghost of Matthew Hopkins is interrogating the Scottish nanny, Carol Compton, but the Ghoul has mixed up her answers! Can you match them with the correct questions? Write a, b, c etc. in the boxes.

a. Are you a nanny? ☐ Yes, I do.
b. Do you come from Scotland? ☐ Yes, I have.
c. Were you arrested for arson and attempted murder? ☐ No, I didn't.
d. Did you try to kill little Agnese? ☐ No, I wasn't.
e. Have you been in prison for 16 months? ☐ Yes, I am.
f. Were you found guilty of witchcraft? ☐ Yes, I was.
g. Are you a witch? ☐ No, I'm not.

27 The Ghoul has eaten some words from these sentences but has left too many spaces. Complete them with *the*, *a*, and *an*, where necessary.

a. Scientists Crick and Watson won .... Nobel Prize for discovering .... genetic code called .... DNA.
b. British schoolchildren can leave .... school at 16.
c. .... witch's 'familiar' is .... demon that takes .... form of .... animal – for example, ... mouse.
d. Matthew Manning can predict .... future.
e. .... *Guardian* contains .... important news.
f. The Ghoul always watches .... 10 o'clock news on .... BBC 1.
g. What did Ruth Lawrence study at .... university?
h. .... boat race is .... annual race on .... Thames from .... Putney Bridge to Mortlake.

➡ Now turn to page 95 for the Revision Test.

Mystery Stop 6

Go north-west from Cambridge.
The city's name has four letters.

The first letter is in 'your' but not in 'our'.
The second letter changes 'put' to 'pot'.
The third letter is in the middle of 'arm'.
The fourth letter comes between 'j' and 'l' in the alphabet.

Now write the name of the city on the map on page **6**.

1 Read the newspaper cuttings and complete the table.

15th July 1979

Famous medium Mrs Doris Stokes claims she 'saw' the Yorkshire Ripper in a vision. 'He is 1.73m tall and slightly-built*,' she said. 'He has a strong, north-east accent – from Newcastle or Sunderland. He is about 23 years old, clean-shaven*, and his hair is light brown or ginger. He works as a builder. He is called "Johnnie" or "Ronnie", and his surname begins with M. He lives alone in a flat over a garage in Sunderland. The street is called Berwick or Bewick.'

3rd January, 1981

Detective Inspector Oldman has released this description of the man arrested yesterday for the Yorkshire Ripper murders.

'His name is Peter Sutcliffe, a 34-year-old lorry driver. He lives in a detached house in Garden Lane, Heaton – a quiet suburb of Bradford, Yorkshire. He is married but has no children.

He is 1.78m tall and has a slim* build. His hair is very dark and he has a thick, dark beard. He speaks with a Yorkshire accent.'

	Mrs Stokes' vision	**The real Yorkshire Ripper**
height		
build	slight	
face	clean-shaven	
hair		
age		
accent		
job		
name		
address		

2 Which one is the Yorkshire Ripper? Tick the correct photo.

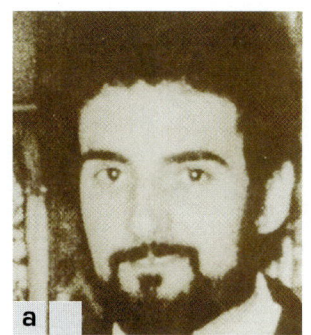

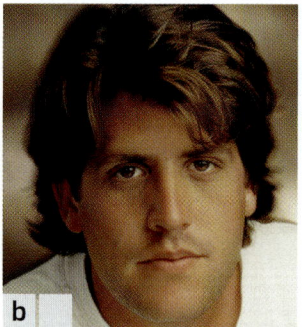

a   b

3 Using information from the table in exercise 1, complete the sentences, like the example.

a. Mrs Stokes said the Ripper was clean-shaven, *but Sutcliffe had a beard.*
b. She said the Ripper lived alone, but ....
c. She said his name was ....
d. She said he had ginger hair ....

Now write your own sentences. Think of address/accent/job etc.

4 Listen to the radio programme report on the Yorkshire Ripper and tick (✓) the correct answers. For question f tick one of the two boxes or complete the third box with your own ideas.

a. The Ripper's reign of terror lasted
   1. ☐ 5 years
   2. ☐ 30 years
   3. ☐ from 1975 to 1981

b. How many women did he kill?
   1. ☐ 7
   2. ☐ 13
   3. ☐ 20

c. During their investigations the police
   1. ☐ interviewed Sutcliffe many times
   2. ☐ arrested Sutcliffe nine times
   3. ☐ suspected Sutcliffe all the time

d. The police finally caught Sutcliffe
   1. ☐ because there was a young woman in his car
   2. ☐ because his car was stolen
   3. ☐ by accident

e. The jury didn't believe that Sutcliffe
   1. ☐ was mad
   2. ☐ was guilty of murder
   3. ☐ should go to prison

f. In my opinion, Sutcliffe was
   1. ☐ mad
   2. ☐ bad
   3. ☐ ....

5 The police received this pretend letter. Complete the spaces with the words provided.

Hello Boss!
It's me – Jack. When are you ¹................. to catch me? If you don't arrest me soon, ²................. lose your job. Do you think you can find me? No, boss, I'm too clever! Every day you ask yourself, 'When and where ³................. kill next?' Let me help you. I'm ⁴................. kill again soon. I haven't decided where, but maybe ⁵................. it in Bradford. Naturally, if the weather ⁶................. bad, I ⁷................. go out. Who knows? Anyway, ⁸................. leave a clue for you – a dead body! Ha, ha! Good luck, boss. Catch me if you can.

Your affectionate friend,
Jack the Ripper

P.S. I'm ⁹................. help you too much!

**is
will he
going to
not going to
I'm going to
you'll
won't
going
I'll do**

6 Use the key words to write sentences with *will* or *going to* in the appropriate column, like the examples.

a. Perhaps/the Ripper/make/a mistake.
b. The Ripper/kill again/soon.
c. Where/the Ripper/kill next?
d. When/the police/catch/the Ripper?
e. The Ripper/not tell/the police/his real plans.

Plans or intentions	Not sure
The police are going to try and find the killer.	Who will be the Ripper's next victim?

7 You have won a lot of money on the lottery. Answer the questions with *will* or *going to*.

a. What are you going to buy first?   I'm not sure. Perhaps ....
   ....

b. Are you going to give anything to your relatives and friends?   Yes, certainly! ....
   ....

c. Are you going to save any of it?   No! ....

d. What will you do if people write to ask you for money?   ....
   ....

6 Mystery History

8 Read the text and write notes for part of the map key (a-f), like example b.

The Industrial Revolution began in the Midlands and North of England in the 18th century. Cotton was the first mechanised industry in the world and Manchester became the first industrial city. In towns like Bolton in Lancashire, the invention of new machines produced cotton faster than before. For example, in 1769 Richard Arkwright of Preston invented the first spinning machine* powered by water. And in 1771 he built the world's first factory in Cromford, Derbyshire. Then in 1781 the world's first steam* engine was built in Birmingham. Four years later Edmund Cartwright of Leicester invented a cotton machine powered by steam. Coal was the fuel* for the new steam engines. People say the Industrial Revolution began at Ironbridge near Birmingham, where Abraham Darby III used coal to build the first iron bridge in the world. Then came the railways…

KEY

a. ....

b. Arkwright's water-powered spinning machine............

c. ....

d. ....

e. ....

f. ....

80

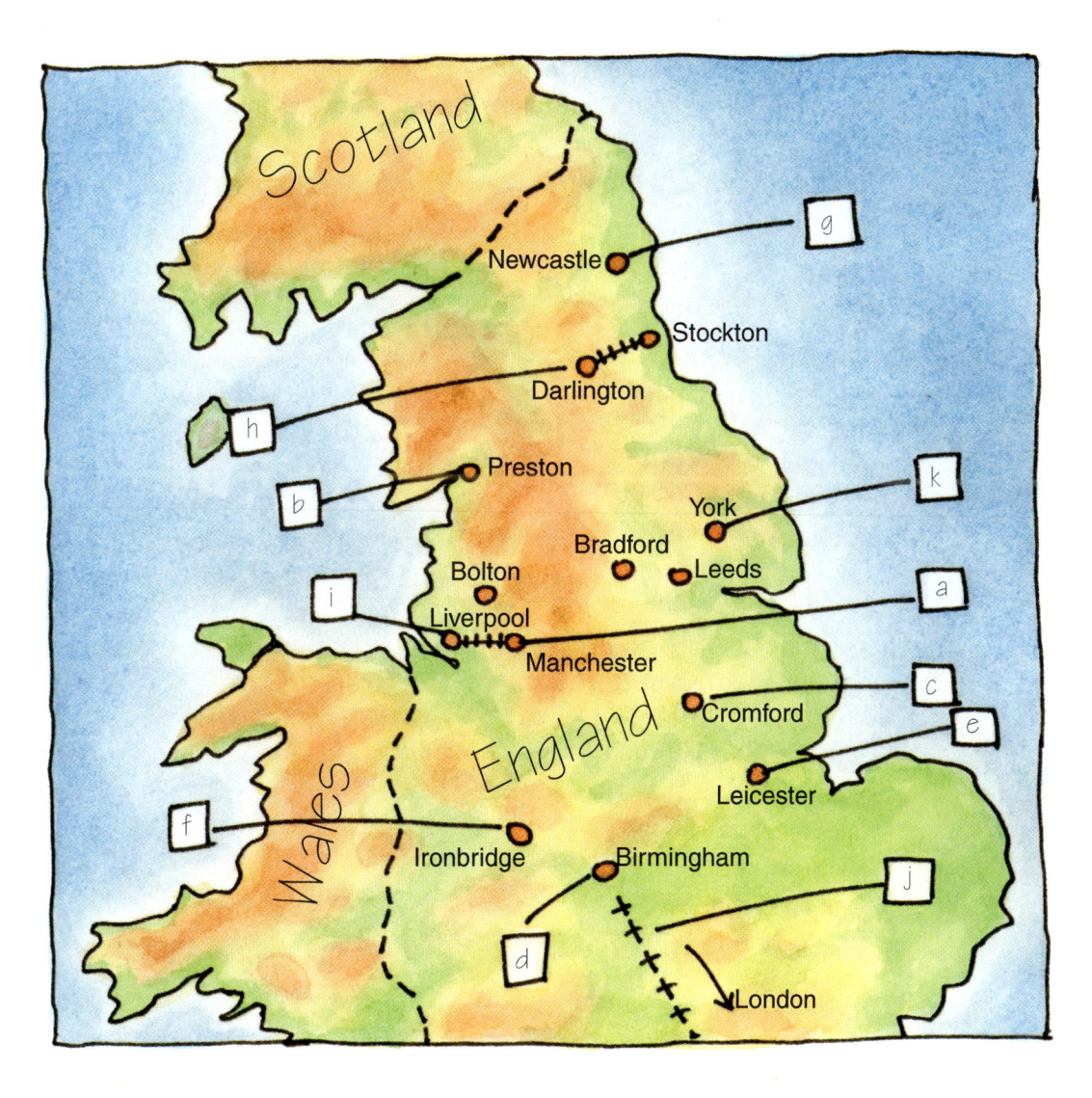

6

g. ....
....

h. ....
....

i. ....
....

j. ....
....

k. ....
....

9 Use the 'railway timetable' to complete the rest of the key (g–k) for the map on the previous page and John Bradford's letter below to his nephew William.

50 YEARS THAT CHANGED THE WORLD

- **1808** Trevithick's first steam locomotive carries passengers at 16 km/hour on a circular railway in London.
- **1814** George Stephenson builds his steam locomotive near Newcastle.
- **1825** Stephenson's engine 'Locomotion' transports coal on the first public railway from Stockton to Darlington.
- **1830** Robert Stephenson's 'Rocket' carries people on the first passenger railway between Liverpool and Manchester.
- **1835** London to Birmingham railway opens.
- **1840s** 'Railway mania'. York becomes a great railway centre. Yorkshire 'Railway King' George Hudson makes a lot of money.
- **1851** 6 million people travel by train to the Great Exhibition in London.

London
May 1st, 1851

Dear William,

I am in London for the ¹................., which is really marvellous. Thousands of people have travelled here by ²................. . Fifty-one years ago, when I was 14 years old, people travelled by coach and horses. Then in ³................. I saw Trevithick's steam locomotive in London. We called it 'Catch-me-who-can'. Many years later – in ⁴................., I think – I travelled on the first passenger railway from ⁵................. to ⁶................. . ⁷................. years later the London to Birmingham railway opened. I remember well the ⁸................. of the 1840s when railways were built everywhere and railway businessmen like ⁹................. became rich. Yes, the world has changed a lot in my lifetime!

Best wishes,
Uncle John

10 What about the next fifty years? Make predictions with the words in the table.

I'm (not) sure		astronauts		destroy	a cure for cancer/AIDS
		we	will	clone	Mars
				dominate	life in the universe
I (don't) think	that	scientists		end	life on earth
		the world	won't	discover	our lives
I (don't) believe		a nuclear war		find	human beings
		computers		travel to	

TIMECHART

11 Read the timechart to do the exercise below.

19th-Century Social Reform

AD
1813   Elizabeth Fry visits Newgate Prison and begins reform of prison conditions, especially for women.
1829   Sir Robert Peel organises the world's first paid police force called 'Peelers'.
1833   Introduction of a 12-hour working day for children under 16 in cotton factories.
1842   Introduction of laws to prohibit women and girls working in coal mines.
1847   Introduction of a 10-hour day for women and children in factories.
1848   Legislation to improve terrible sanitary conditions of the poor.
1855   First nursing system organised by Florence Nightingale in Turkey during Crimean War.
1867   Dr Thomas Barnardo founds homes for destitute children.
1882   Legislation provides more economic freedom to women.
1891   School is free to all children.

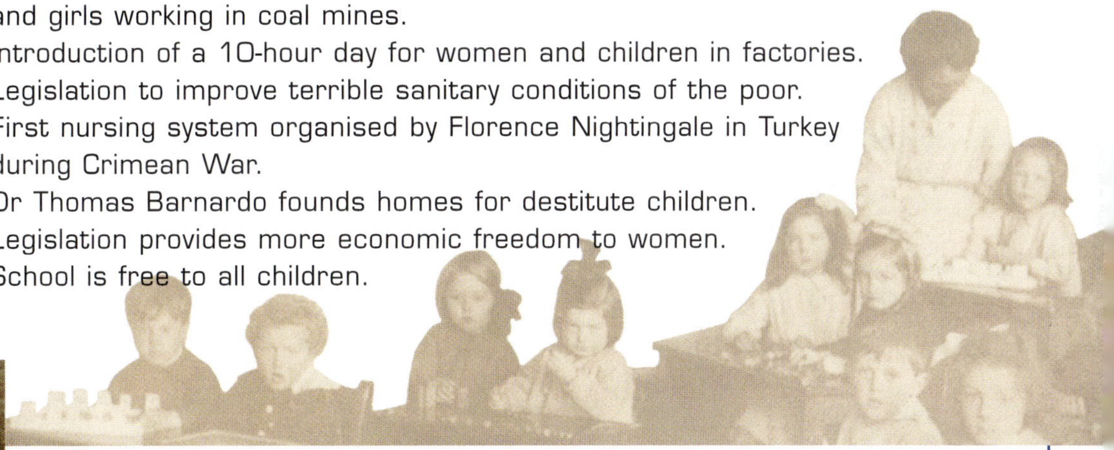

Peel's 'Peelers'.

12 Underline the correct word.

    a. Before 1833, children worked *more/fewer* than 12 hours a day in factories.
    b. After 1842 *boys/girls* over 10 still worked in coal mines.
    c. 'Peelers' was a new name for professional *nurses/policemen*.
    d. Before 1891 people *paid/didn't pay* for education.
    e. *Elizabeth Fry/Florence Nightingale* looked after wounded soldiers, who called her 'the lady with the lamp'.
    f. In the 1880s women had *less/more* freedom than before.

Write a similar sentence of your own for the year 1847.

....
....
....

Florence Nightingale.

18th-century workers. Joseph Wright of Derby (1734-97).

6

Britain – The Mother of Invention

13 Complete the information about some British inventions with the words provided.

> stamp   football   Christopher   telephone   railway
> invented   rugby   Wimbledon   photography   transport
> television   1930   cricket

SPORT

- ¹..................... is a type of football. Players can kick the ball or run with it.
- The first international tennis tournament was held at ²..................... in 1877.
- ³..................... is a popular summer sport played with a bat and ball.
- The rules of ⁴..................... were made in 1848.

COMMUNICATIONS

1835 W. H. Fox Talbot invented the negative/positive process in ⁵..................... . He made the first photo negative.

1840 First postage ⁶..................... invented by Rowland Hill.

1876 Briton Alexander Graham Bell invented the ⁷..................... in America.

1926 First ⁸..................... transmission by John Logie Baird.

(1936 First public TV service by BBC)

⁹.............................

- First underground ¹⁰..................... – The Metropolitan Line – opened in 1863.
- First pedal-powered bicycle was ¹¹..................... by Kirkpatrick Macmillan in 1839.
- Frank Whittle invented the jet engine in ¹²..................... .
- The hovercraft was invented in 1955 by ¹³..................... Cockerell.

14 The sentences are in chronological order.
Write the correct year in the spaces.

MEDICINE

¹....................: Edward Jenner invents the vaccination, a type of inoculation.
²....................: James Simpson first uses chloroform, an early anaesthetic. Queen Victoria takes it during childbirth in ³.................... .
⁴....................: Joseph Lister introduces use of antiseptics in Glasgow.
⁵....................: Alexander Fleming discovers penicillin, the first antibiotic.

1865, 1928, 1853, 1796, 1847

15 Discovery or invention?
Complete the sentences with the correct form of *discover/invent*.

SCIENCE AND TECHNOLOGY

- Joseph Priestley ¹.................... oxygen in 1774.
- In 1882 Charles Babbage ².................... an automatic calculating machine – an early computer.
- Michael Faraday – the father of modern technology – ³.................... the electric current in 1831. This led to many ⁴...................., like the electric light.
- J. J. Thomson ⁵.................... the electron in 1897.
- Radar was ⁶.................... by Robert Watson-Watt in 1935.

Write a list of inventions/discoveries from your country.

....
....
....
....

6

16 Complete the advertisements for Professor Goon's new inventions with the words below.

   a. These square glasses give you perfect vision for watching all types of TV.
   b. This makes you white and can change you into a lunatic!
   c. Just put your head on the block and release the spring.
   d. Just aim and fire – then watch them drop!

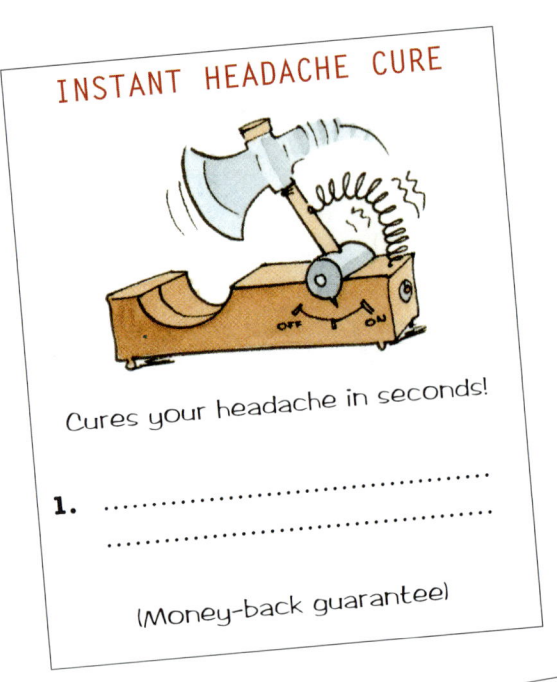

INSTANT HEADACHE CURE

Cures your headache in seconds!

1. ....

(Money-back guarantee)

SPECIALLY ADAPTED FOR TV

No more viewing problems!

2. ....

(As advertised on TV)

YOU CAN'T MISS! IT'S EASY WITH THE NEW MOSQUITO-SHOOTER

Say goodbye to creams and sprays.

3. ....

(Also effective for killing flies and wasps)

ORGANIC NON-GREASY MOON LOTION

Protects you from moonlight.

4. ....

(Warning. This product becomes toxic in starlight)

Pen and Ink Link

17 First, look carefully at the grid. Then listen and complete it, as shown.

	Charlotte	Emily	Anne
born 1816			
Wuthering Heights			
lived in Haworth	✓	✓	✓
died 1855			
youngest sister			
The Tenant of Wildfell Hall			
born 1818			
Jane Eyre			
genius			
eldest sister			
died at the age of 30			

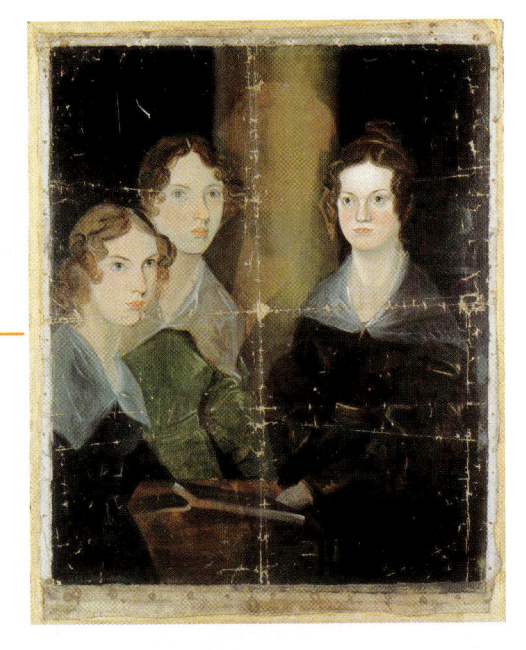

The Brontë Sisters by Patrick Branwell Brontë (1817-48).
By courtesy of the National Portrait Gallery, London.

The ruins of a house which is said to have been the setting for *Wuthering Heights*.

6

18 The Yorkshire Moors are wild and beautiful, but England has a lot of environmental problems. Here are some below. Complete the *For/Against* boxes with sentences a-g. Write a, b, c etc. in the appropriate column.

	For	Against
Chemical fertilisers and genetically-modified crops in farming →	Bigger, cheaper crops*, free of disease*.	1. ....
Factories →	2.	Create industrial waste*. Consume too much raw* material.
More roads →	Goods transported quickly. People can travel to more places.	3. ....
Packaging →	4.	Creates litter*. Difficult to dispose of* plastics, etc.
More electricity and power →	Necessary for heating, TV and other household things.	5. ....
More new houses, offices etc. →	6.	Building uses too much land and destroys the countryside.
Tourism →	People enjoy visiting places. Makes a lot of money.	7. ....

a. Traffic fumes pollute* the air. Traffic congestion. Road accidents.
b. Too many people create noise and litter, and ruin the beauty of the environment.
c. People need modern homes, offices and shops.
d. Provide employment* and make useful things.
e. Power stations pollute the atmosphere and cause acid rain. Dangers of nuclear power.
f. Danger to wildlife and rivers. Food safety.
g. Protects products like food and hi-fi equipment.

The Word Wizard

19 The Wizard has made a puzzle of popular British sports and activities. Complete the puzzle and find the mystery word.

CLUES

1. You can do this in the sea or in the pool.
2. You play this in summer with a bat and ball.
3. It begins with 'w.' You only need two legs to do it.
4. You ride your bike in the mountains.
5. People do these exercises with music to keep fit.
6. It's a pub game with a green table and balls.
7. OFGL. It's a popular sport with businessmen.
8. Let's go .... at the disco.
9. The most popular pub game.
10. You need a garden to do this.
11. You catch a water animal with a rod* and line*.
12. Horse ....
13. You can do this with a bicycle.

The mystery word is ....

6

The Grammar Ghoul

20 Underline the correct form of the verbs.

a. Peter Sutcliffe said, 'If they *will think/think* I'm mad, *I/I'll* only get 10 years in hospital.'
b. Detective Oldman *loses/will lose* his job if he *doesn't/won't* catch the killer.
c. What *do/will* astronauts find if they *will travel/travel* to Mars?
d. If scientists *will discover/discover* a cure for cancer, it *saves/will save* many lives.
e. Our countryside *won't be/isn't* beautiful in future if we *continue/will continue* to build more houses and factories.
f. *Do/Will* you go out if the weather *is/will be* fine tomorrow?

21 The Ghoul is writing a book about the Yorkshire Ripper but he has forgotten to include these important words. Write the correct word from the box below in the spaces.

Peter Sutcliffe was a serial killer. ¹.................... victims were all women and some of ².................... were prostitutes. During ³.................... investigations the police interviewed ⁴.................... many times but ⁵.................... didn't think ⁶.................... was the Ripper. Then in 1981 a policeman saw Sutcliffe in a car with a young woman. Sutcliffe told ⁷.................... to say that ⁸.................... was ⁹.................... girlfriend. Then he got out of the car and hid a hammer and a knife in some bushes. The policeman asked Sutcliffe if the car was ¹⁰.................... and he said yes.
'¹¹.................... number plates* are false,' said the policeman. '¹².................... must come with ¹³.................... to the police station.' Later, the policeman went back and found Sutcliffe's weapons.
'Are these ¹⁴....................?' the police asked.
'Yes, they're ¹⁵....................,' Sutcliffe replied. '¹⁶.................... am the Yorkshire Ripper.'
The police told reporters, '¹⁷.................... have found the man called the Yorkshire Ripper. After 5½ years ¹⁸.................... investigations are finally over.'

his	them	they	our	yours	she
him	you	I	her	his	your	me
their	we	he	mine	his	

➡ Now turn to page 95 for the Revision Test.

Revision Tests

Mystery Stop 1 (pages 7-20)

1 Complete the sentences with the verbs in the brackets. Use the Present Simple or Continuous tense.

a. Look there's a ghost! It .... (*walk*) through the wall.
b. Why .... you .... (*wear*) your gloves? It isn't cold.
c. English people .... (*eat*) too many cakes and sweets.
d. Kevin and Susan .... (*not make*) a model of Versailles now.
e. The lady in grey .... (*not haunt*) Popjoy's restaurant.

2 Disagree with these statements.

Example: *The ghost in Saville Row wears an orange hat.* No, he doesn't.

a. Kevin and Susan aren't making a model of Buckingham Palace. ....
b. Juliana Popjoy haunts the Garrick's Head pub. ....
c. The grandfather clock on page 9 isn't striking 13. ....
d. Admiral Philip doesn't make strange noises. ....
e. English people don't use their cars very much. ....
f. We go to a bookshop to borrow books. ....
g. The two hands on page 9 are playing a violin. ....
h. Bath is in the north of England. ....

3 Underline the correct words in the questions and answers.

a. How **much/many** eggs have we got in the fridge?   Only **a few/a little**.
b. How **much/many** fruit did the Celts eat?   Just **a few/a little**.
c. How **much/many** spaghetti would you like?   **A few/a little**, please.
d. How **much/many** money have you won?   Just **a few/a little**.
e. How **much/many** sandwiches shall I make?   Just **a few/a little**.

4 Complete the text with the correct preposition.

> from   at   in   near   on (x2)

Bath is a city ¹............... south-west England. It's situated ²............... the River Avon, not far ³............... Bristol. In 43 AD the Romans landed ⁴............... a port ⁵............... the south-east coast and conquered Britain. They built a town and baths ⁶............... a sacred spring of hot water called Sulis, which became the modern city of Bath.

Mystery Stop 2 (pages 21-34)

1 Complete the questions and answers with the correct form of the verbs in the box. Look at the example.

> see   have   shine   fall   ~~grow~~   hear   think

Example: *Did some flowers **grow** nearly 12 metres tall in Warminster?
No, they **grew** nearly 4 metres tall.*

a. Did some pigeons .... from the trees in Warminster?
No, they .... from the sky.
b. Did Willy Gehlen .... a ticking sound?
No, he .... a humming sound.
c. Did Mrs Attwell .... an object in the sea?
No, she .... it in the sky.
d. Did the alien .... green hair?
No, it .... yellow hair.
e. Did Gehlen .... the alien was a soldier?
No, he .... it was a farmer.
f. Did the alien .... the spaceship lights at Gehlen?
No, it .... a torch.

2 Complete the sentences with the Past Simple (negative/positive) form of the verbs in the box. Look at the example.

> begin   ~~live~~   know   write   win   build   become

Example: *The Buddha **didn't live** in the 20th century. He **lived** in the 6th century.*

a. The Ancient Britons .... about the wheel. They .... about Greek mathematics.
b. Becket .... a saint in 1170. He .... a saint in 1173.
c. Bishop Poore .... a letter to Henry VIII. He .... it to Henry III.
d. Rastafarianism .... in the 6th century. It .... in the 1920s.
e. The Romans .... Stonehenge. The Ancient Britons .... it.
f. Italy .... the World Cup in 1966. England .... it.

3 Underline the correct preposition.

a. Roger Rump woke up early **in/on/at** Christmas Day.
b. The Thing made contact with humans **in/on/at** 1976.
c. Willy Gehlen was woken by a humming sound **in/on/at** 3am.

d. Work began on Stonehenge **at/about/on** 2800 BC.
e. Work began on Salisbury Cathedral **in/at/on** April, 1220.
f. The Buddha lived **on/at/in** the 6th century.
g. Midsummer Day is **in/at/on** June 21st.
h. **In/At/On** autumn 1979 Cardinal Wojtyla became Pope.

Mystery Stop 3 (pages 35-48)

1 Underline the correct verb tense.

a. A photographer **was dying/died** suddenly when he **took/was taking** pictures of the mummy-case.
b. Douglas Murray **shot/was shooting** crocodiles when his gun **exploded/was exploding**.
c. Murray's friends **died/were dying** mysteriously when they **were going/went** back to England.
d. Francis Drake **played/was playing** a game of bowls when the Spanish Armada **was arriving/arrived**.
e. Robinson Crusoe **was sailing/sailed** to Africa when he **was/was being** shipwrecked on an island.

2 Complete the sentences with the appropriate form of 'to be'. Then match them with the adjectives. Write a, b, c etc. in the boxes.

a. What .... the weather like yesterday? ☐ Fascinating.
b. What .... the pyramids like? ☐ Poor.
c. What .... the Bristol Sound like? ☐ Cold.
d. What .... the first American immigrants like? ☐ Loud.

3 Complete the superlative sentences with 'the most' and an appropriate adjective, like the example.

romantic   delicious   beautiful   interesting   ~~incredible~~   exciting   fantastic

Example: *'Princess of Death' is the most **incredible** story I've heard.*

a. *Robinson Crusoe* is .... book I've read.
b. Paris is .... city I've visited.
c. India is .... country I've seen.
d. The Italians are .... people in the world.
e. *Titanic* is .... film I've seen.
f. Chinese food is .... food I've eaten.

Mystery Stop 4 (pages 49-62)

1 Complete the questions with the Past Simple or Present Perfect form of the verbs in brackets.

a. .... the Labour Party .... the general election in 1997? (*win*)
b. .... any strange things .... recently at 50 Berkeley Square? (*happen*)
c. .... Anne Boleyn .... the Tower since 1536? (*haunt*)
d. .... Charles Dickens .... London well? (*know*)
e. .... you .... to the London Dungeon yet? (*be*)
f. .... the show already ....? (*finish*)

2 *Since* or *for*? Underline the correct word.

a. I've had nightmares **since/for** I saw the ghost.
b. Kings and queens have been crowned in Westminster Abbey **since/for** 1066.
c. The strange happenings have continued **since/for** six months.
d. Catherine Howard has walked the walls of the Tower **since/for** over 400 years.
e. Millions of people have visited Madame Tussaud's **since/for** it opened in 1835.

3 Complete the text with the words in the box.

> but (x2)   then   because   so
> since   when   and   for   where

The most haunted house in England is Borley Rectory. There have been hundreds of reports of mysterious happenings ¹.................... it was built in 1863. Many people believe the Borley ghost is Marie Lairre ².................... her husband murdered her in 1667 at the place ³.................... the Rectory was later built. A woman's skeleton was discovered under the ruins in 1943 ⁴.................... everyone said it must be Marie Lairre. ⁵.................... some people think it was only the skeleton of a victim of the plague. In 1929 poltergeist activity began ⁶.................... the owners sold the house in 1930 to the Foyster family. They moved out quickly ⁷.................... an invisible entity attacked Mrs Foyster. ⁸.................... the Rectory was destroyed by fire in 1939. The building has gone ⁹.................... its supernatural residents are still there. People have reported seeing them ¹⁰.................... many years.

Mystery Stop 5 (pages 63-76)

1 Complete the questions with the words in the box.

> When   Why   How   Who   Where   What

a. .... wrote *Alice in Wonderland*?
b. .... was Carol Compton released immediately?
c. .... is the witch's mark?
d. .... did Crick and Watson discuss DNA?
e. .... was *The Origin of Species* published?
f. .... do most English people spend their free time?

2 Do these 'can' questions refer to ability (A) or permission (P)? Put A or P in the boxes. Then write suitable short answers, like *Yes, he can/No, he can't*.

a. Can British schoolchildren leave school when they are 16?   ☐ ....
b. Can Matthew Manning heal sick people?   ☐ ....
c. Can most people get a mathematics degree when they are 12?   ☐ ....
d. Can British children start primary school when they are 2?   ☐ ....
e. Can Carol Compton make herself invisible?   ☐ ....

3 Underline the appropriate word.

a. Cromwell's head was **built/buried** in Sussex College chapel.
b. Carol Compton was **hanged/arrested** on the island of Elba.
c. Matthew Manning's psychic powers were **investigated/released** in 1974.
d. The Senate House was **built/published** in the 18th century.
e. The laws of gravity were **executed/discovered** by Newton.
f. Carol Compton was **founded/found** guilty of arson.

Mystery Stop 6 (pages 77-90)

1 These sentences express prediction or intention. Complete them with the verbs in brackets. Use *will/won't* for predictions and *(not) going to* for intentions or plans.

a. 'I believe the murderer .... (*strike*) again next week in Newcastle,' said Doris Stokes.
b. 'We .... (*try*) very hard to catch the murderer,' said Chief Inspector Oldman.

c. 'Tomorrow it .... (*be*) cold but it ....
(*not rain*),' said the weatherman.

d. 'I've made a New Year's resolution,' said my friend. 'I ....
(*stop*) smoking.'

e. Friends of the Earth say that if we continue to use chemicals in farming, our food .... (*be*) too contaminated to eat.

f. 'We want to protect the environment so we .... (*not build*) any more new roads,' said the Transport Minister.

g. In his letter to the police the killer wrote, 'I .... (*kill*) again very soon and I'm sure you .... (*not catch*) me – not in a million years!'

2 Complete the text with the words in the box.

> suburb   as a builder   divorced   flat   built
> Scottish accent   ginger   beard   32 years   1.80m tall

Superintendant Ron Barker gave this description of the murderer. 'He is
¹.................... old and about ².................... . He is well-³.................... . His hair is ⁴.................... and he has a thick ⁵.................... . He speaks with a strong ⁶.................... . He lives in a ⁷.................... in a ⁸.................... of Glasgow, where he works ⁹.................... . He has two children but he is ¹⁰.................... and lives alone.'

3 Use the verbs in the box to complete the sentences. Think about the verb tenses!

> destroy   investigate   discover   invent
> predict   speak   pollute   arrest   provide

a. The police .... Peter Sutcliffe in Sheffield.
b. Alexander Graham Bell .... the telephone.
c. The murderer .... with a Yorkshire accent.
d. Traffic fumes .... the atmosphere.
e. Four hundred years ago Nostradamus .... the future in his work *Centuries*.
f. Industrial waste from factories .... wildlife and the countryside.
g. The police .... the murder of a young woman in Manchester.
h. Power stations .... electricity for our homes.
i. Who .... penicillin?